High-Impact Tools for Teams

Published by John Wiley & Sons, Inc., Hoboken, New Jersey.
Published simultaneously in Canada.

For general information on our other products and services or for technical support, please contact our Customer Care Department within the United States at (800) 762-2974, outside the United States at (317) 572-3993 or fax (317) 572-4002.

Wiley publishes in a variety of print and electronic formats and by print-on-demand. Some material included with standard print versions of this book may not be included in e-books or in print-on-demand. If this book refers to media such as a CD or DVD that is not included in the version you purchased, you may download this material at http://booksupport.wiley.com. For more information about Wiley products, visit www.wiley.com.

Library of Congress Cataloging-in-Publication Data:
ISBN 9781119602385 (Paperback)
ISBN 9781119602804 (ePDF)
ISBN 9781119602811 (ePub)

Cover illustration: Blexbolex
Cover design: Alan Smith

SKY10022567_111720

You're holding a powerful toolkit to
create alignment, build trust, and get results fast.
Rediscover the joy of teamwork with these five...

High-Impact Tools for Teams

strategyzer.com/teams

Written by
Stefano Mastrogiacomo
Alex Osterwalder

Designed by
Alan Smith
Trish Papadakos

WILEY

"Management is about human beings. Its task is to make people capable of joint performance."

Peter Drucker, Management Thinker

Contents

+

Essentials
What makes teams
underperform and how
to get better results
p. 1

Discover the Team Alignment Map
What it is and how it works

2

Put the Map into Action
How to use the
Team Alignment Map

3

Trust Among Team Members
Four tools to create a high-trust
climate and increased
psychological safety

4

Dive Deeper
Discover the science behind
the tools and the book

Foreword

Amy Edmondson

If you are leading a team – or plan to any-time soon – you'll want to keep this book close at hand. Most leaders today recognize that their organizations are deeply dependent on teams to accelerate innovation and digitalization, address changing customer demands, and cope with sudden disruptive events such as the global pandemic, social unrest, and recession.

But just putting a team together does not ensure its success. Teams fail on a regular basis. Launched with a meaningful goal, the right people to accomplish it, and even sufficient resources, time and time again, teams nevertheless struggle to deliver on their undeniable potential. They get bogged down by coordination lapses, ineffective meetings, unproductive conflicts, and dysfunctional group dynamics – leading to frustration, delays, and flawed decisions. Researchers call these factors "process losses" – in an effort to explain the gap between inputs (skills, goals, and resources) and outcomes (team performance or member satisfaction). Even when teams seem to get work done, their performance may be suboptimal – conventional rather than innovative, or come at a cost of high levels of overwork, stress, and disengagement.

It doesn't have to be this way.

Stefano Mastrogiacomo and Alex Osterwalder show us how teams can thrive by using simple practices that work. They offer a playbook any team can use to immediately put itself on a path to full participation, productive conflict, and steady progress. With its engaging illustrations, accessible tools, and thoughtful sequences of activities that teams can use to avoid (and recover from) predictable team problems of all sorts, this book is an invaluable resource. I have long believed that simple tools can bring synergy within reach by nudging team behavior in the right direction. And this book is full of such tools – activities and guidelines that will serve any team well.

Yet, what is particularly powerful about *High Impact Tools for Teams* is its emphasis on team process and the psychological climate. Most authors address one or the other – offering a step-by-step guide to manage a team project or else explaining the benefits of a psychologically safe climate that allows teams to learn and innovate.

This book offers simple tools to do both. When speaking up in a team is thwarted by a poor climate, innovation suffers, problems fester and sometimes turn into major failures. But creating psychological safety can sound like an elusive goal, especially for team leaders under pressure to deliver results. Drawing from my research, and that of so many others whose work underpins this terrific resource, Stefano and Alex demystify the quest for a healthy team culture – and walk us through how to create it. For this reason alone, I'm excited about this book. It injects new energy – and new tools – into the quest to build teams that can thrive in the 21st century by fully engaging the energy and expertise of all who work in them.

Even if teamwork will always be challenging, leaders now have access to practical, easy-to-use tools to help teams work well. Leaders who adopt them with passionate intent will be poised to build the kind of teams that companies need and employees want.

– Amy C. Edmondson
Harvard Business School, Cambridge, MA

Seven Great Thinkers
Who Inspired This Book

Herbert Clark

Herbert H. Clark is a psycholinguist and professor of psychology at Stanford University. The very foundations of this book lie in his works on language use in human coordination. The design of the **Team Alignment Map** is inspired by his research on mutual understanding and the coordination of joint activities.

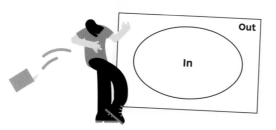

Yves Pigneur

Yves Pigneur is professor of management and information systems at the University of Lausanne, Switzerland. His work in design thinking and tool design helped us bridge the difficult gap between theory and practice. Without his conceptual support and guidance, this book and all the tools it contains would simply not exist.

Alan Fiske

Alan Page Fiske is professor of psychological anthropology at the University of California, Los Angeles. His works on the nature of human relationships and cross-cultural variations have disrupted our understanding of what "social" means and resulted in the actual design of the **Team Contract**.

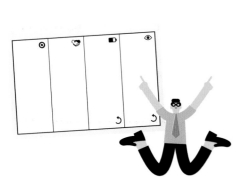

Amy Edmondson

Amy Edmondson is professor of leadership and management at the Harvard Business School. The integration of the four add-ons has been influenced by her work on trust in teams, in particular the notion of psychological safety among team members. Her research provided us with great insight in understanding the impact of trust in cross-functional teamwork and on innovation.

Steven Pinker

Steven Pinker is professor of psychology at Harvard. His works on psycholinguistics and social relations, in particular the use of indirect language and polite requests in cooperative games, inspired the design of the **Respect Card**. His recent works on common knowledge shape our future developments.

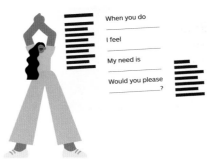

Françoise Kourilsky

Françoise Kourilsky is a psychologist and coach specializing in change management. She pioneered the introduction of systemics and brief therapy techniques to manage change in organization, working directly with Paul Watzlawick of the Mental Research Institute, Palo Alto, California. We owe her the **Fact Finder**, which is a new interpretation of her "language compass."

Marshall Rosenberg

Marshall Rosenberg was a psychologist, mediator, and author. He founded the Center for Nonviolent Communication and worked worldwide as a peacemaker. His work on the language of conflict resolution and empathetic communication inspired the design of the **Nonviolent Requests Guide**.

Meet the Strategyzer Series

We believe that simple, visual, practical tools can transform the effectiveness of a person, a team, and their organization. While new business ideas fail, existing businesses are under constant threat of disruption and obsolescence. Unacceptable amounts of time and money are lost each year due to lack of clarity and alignment on fundamental business issues. Each of our books has a set of purpose-built tools and processes to tackle specific challenges. These challenges are interconnected, so we've meticulously designed the tools to stand on their own and integrate with each other to create the world's most integrated strategy and innovation toolkit. Get one or get them all, either way — you'll get results.

strategyzer.com/books

Business Model Generation

A handbook for visionaries, game changers, and challengers striving to defy outmoded business models and design tomorrow's enterprises. Adapt to harsh new realities and get out in front of your competitors with *Business Model Generation*.

Value Proposition Design

Tackle the core challenge of every business — creating compelling products and services customers want to buy. Discover a repeatable process and the right tools to create products that sell.

Testing Business Ideas

Discover a library of 44 experiments to systematically test your business ideas. Combine the Business Model Canvas and Value Proposition Canvas with Assumptions Mapping and other powerful lean startup tools.

The Invincible Company

Become unstoppable by simultaneously managing a portfolio of existing businesses and exploring a pipeline of potential new growth engines. Discover practical and essential tools including the Business Portfolio Map, Innovation Metrics, the Culture Map, and a library of Business Model Patterns.

High-Impact Tools for Teams

Five powerful teamwork and change management tools to successfully implement new business models. Make every innovation project a success with the Team Alignment Map, the Team Contract, the Fact Finder, the Respect Card, and the Nonviolent Requests Guide.

Essentials

What makes teams underperform and how to get better results

"Talk is the technology of leadership."

Jeanne Liedtka, Strategist

Our people are top-notch.

So, how come we have all these problems?

When was the last time you enjoyed contributing to a team?

$37B

is the salary cost in USD of unnecessary meetings for U.S. businesses.

Atlassian *

50%

of meetings are considered unproductive and a waste of time.

Atlassian *

29%

of projects are successful.

*Chaos Report,
The Standish Group, 2019*

75%

of cross-functional teams are dysfunctional.

Behnam Tabrizi, "75% of Cross-Functional Teams Are Dysfunctional,"

Harvard Business Review, 2015

10%

of team members
agree about who is on
their team (120 teams).

Diane Coutu, "Why Teams Don't Work,"
Harvard Business Review, 2009

66%

of U.S. workers are not
engaged or are actively
disengaged at work.

*Jim Harter, Gallup, 2018 ***

95%

of a company's
employees are
unaware of, or
do not understand,
its strategy.

Robert Kaplan and David Norton,
"The Office of Strategy Management,"
Harvard Business Review, 2005

1/3

of value-added
collaborations come
from only 3% to 5%
of employees.

Rob Cross, Reb Rebele, and
Adam Grant, "Collaborative
Overload," Harvard Business Review,
2016

* "You Waste a Lot of Time at Work," Atlassian, www.atlassian.com/time-wasting-at-work-infographic
** "Employee Engagement on the Rise in the U.S.," Gallup, news.gallup.com/poll/241649/employee-engagement-rise.aspx

What Makes Teams Underperform

Teams underperform when members work *around* each other and not *with* each other, something that happens when the team climate is unsafe and the team activities are poorly aligned.

Working around each other is an exhausting journey. Endless meetings and skyrocketing budgets for poor results usually occur in a poor team climate where most members work under high pressure and feel isolated and unhappy. This is the daily life of many team members, without caricaturing things as surveys illustrate.

We are capable of doing more than merely work around each other. We can work with each other, for real. When this happens we can accomplish the nearly impossible with passion. We may not necessarily realize it but in that moment, we are experiencing a "high-performing team." Something people coin in retrospect because good results gradually add up.

We have experienced both types of teams, and this book contains what we have learned over the past 20 years. Our key learning is that joint success and failure largely depend on how well we manage our day-to-day interactions, at two levels:

- The team activities: having an obsession for mutual clarity — what's the mission, who is doing what, is it clear for everyone?
- The team climate: carefully nurturing strong, trust-based relationships.

We believe in teams and we believe in tools. This is why we spent the past five years designing and revamping tools that do just that. Tools that help team members improve:

1. the team activities through better team alignment, and
2. the team climate by building psychologically safer work environments.

Only teams can tackle the complexity of the challenges brought by an interconnected world. We're going through a period of spectacular changes: game-changing technologies and unprecedented lockdowns are disrupting entire industries. Organizations are forced to innovate and deliver at an unprecedented pace, and teams are, for us, the building block. The need to revisit the way we work together has never been greater.

As the visionary Peter Drucker announced long ago: The critical question is not "How can I achieve?" but "What can I contribute?" We couldn't agree more. We hope the Team Alignment Map and the other tools presented in this book help you as much as they help us become better team contributors, every day.

Unsafe Team Climate
Signs of a poor team climate

- Lack of trust between colleagues and teams
- Internal competition
- Disengagement
- Lack of recognition
- Fear: it's difficult to speak up
- Over-collaboration
- Lost joy of working together

Misaligned Team Activities
Signs of poor alignment of team activities

- It's unclear who does what
- Invaluable time is lost in endless meetings
- Work is delivered too slowly
- Priorities keep changing and no one can figure out why
- Duplicate projects and projects overlap
- Team members work in silos
- A lot of work is done with poor results and little impact

Activities Get Stuck in Misaligned Teams

In concrete terms, alignment is communicating to create common ground, common knowledge, shared or mutual understanding (all used as synonyms in this book — Dive Deeper, p. 252). Common ground enables team members to anticipate the actions of others and act accordingly through aligned predictions. The richer a team's common ground, the better the mutual predictions between team members and the overall execution, thanks to a seamless division of labor and a consistent integration of the individual parts. Interestingly, conversation — face-to-face dialogue — is still the most effective technology on Earth to build relevant common ground.

Adapted from: Herbert H. Clark, Using Language (Cambridge University Press, 1996). Simon Garrod and Martin J. Pickering, "Joint Action, Interactive Alignment, and Dialogue," Topics in Cognitive Science 1, no. 2 (2009): 292–304.

How Team Alignment Works

Successful alignment
Anything teams achieve, from having a party to building an airplane, is a by-product of team alignment. Alignment is the process of making individual contributions converge to achieve a shared goal for mutual benefit. It transforms individuals going about their business into successful team contributors. Working in a team requires more effort than working alone; team members must constantly synchronize with each other in addition to doing their own part of the work. The payoff is achieving (greater) goals that can't be accomplished alone.

Cooperation for Mutual Outcome

Unsuccessful alignment
Expect only poor results from a misaligned team. Unsuccessful communication prevents the creation of relevant common ground; participants do not understand each other and mispredict each other's actions. This causes team members to carry out tasks with important perception gaps. The division of work and the integration of the individual parts goes off track and the lack of collaboration is inefficient and costly. The intended results are not achieved as expected.

Successful communication
Team members openly exchange relevant information.

Relevant common ground
Mutual understanding is established among team members; they are aligned on what needs to be achieved and how.

Effective coordination
Team members make successful predictions about each other; coordination is harmonious and individual contributions integrate successfully.

Mutual benefit

Communication
Information team members share verbally and non-verbally, synchronously and asynchronously.

Common Ground
Knowledge team members know they have in common, also known as common knowledge or mutual knowledge.

Coordination
Tasks team members need to perform to work together harmoniously.

Outcome

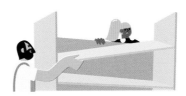

Unsuccessful communication
Team members do not exchange relevant information.

Low or irrelevant common ground
Perception gaps build up while team members execute their individual parts.

Coordination surprises
Individual contributions are not integrated with one another. Bad surprises accumulate due to inefficient coordination.

Mutual loss

An Unsafe Team Climate Undermines Innovation

I feel insecure: I don't want to look ignorant, incompetent, intrusive, or negative. Better to not take risks.

I stay silent and don't share crucial information

Adapted from Amy Edmondson, "Psychological Safety and Learning Behavior in Work Teams," *Administrative Science Quarterly* 44, no. 2 (1999): 350–383.

Psychologically unsafe environment

Team members protect themselves from embarrassment and other possible threats by remaining silent when the climate is psychologically unsafe. The team doesn't engage in collective learning behaviors and that results in poor team performance.

+
No learning behaviors

Low common ground
The team's common ground (or common knowledge) is not updated. Perception gaps increase between team members and the team relies on outdated information.

↓

Low team learning
Habitual or automatic behaviors keep being repeated, despite changes in context.

↓

Low team performance
Assumptions are not revised and plans are not corrected. The work performed is not in line with the actual situation and the delivered outcomes become inadequate.

↓

Status quo or worse

I am confident that
errors won't be held
against me. I respect
and I feel respected by
my team.

**I speak up and share
crucial information**

Psychologically safe environment

Team members are not afraid to
speak up when the climate is psychologically safe. Team members
engage in a productive dialogue
that fosters the proactive learning
behaviors required to understand the
environment and the clients and solve
problems together efficiently.

+
Learning behaviors

Seeking feedback

Sharing info

Asking for help

Talking about errors

Experimenting

High common ground
The team's common ground (or
common knowledge) is regularly
updated with new and fresh
information.
↓

High team learning
New information helps the team
learn and adapt. Learning behaviors help the team make changes
in assumptions and plans.
↓

High team performance
Open communications help the
team coordinate effectively.
Constant integration of learnings
and adaptation to changes in the
context result in relevant work.

↓
Complex
problem-solving

The new hire will solve all our problems.

How Alignment and Safety Affect Team Impact

Today's challenges are too daunting for isolated talents working in pseudo teams. Complex problem solving requires real teamwork and that starts by building solid team alignment and a safe climate.

Low Effort Toward Mission

Low Ability to Achieve

× Misaligned Activities
× Unsafe Climate

Low Effort Toward Mission

High Ability to Achieve

× Misaligned Activities
√ Safe Climate

High Effort Toward Mission

Some Ability to Achieve

√ Aligned Activities
× Unsafe Climate

Best Effort Toward Mission

Best Ability to Achieve

√ Aligned Activities
√ Safe Climate

Impact

The Team Alignment Map Solution

Increase alignment and trust in your teams with the Team Alignment Map (TAM) and its four add-ons. They're simple, practical, and easy to implement.

Clarify and align every team member's contribution to the TAM in planning mode. A simple two-step process (named the forward pass and backward pass) facilitates planning and helps reduce risks.

Also use the TAM in assessment mode, for rapidly assessing teams and projects. Assessments are performed on the same canvas by adding four scales on which the team can vote, think, and act.

Improves Activities
Improves Climate

Improve team activities

Use the Team Alignment Map to align the team activities

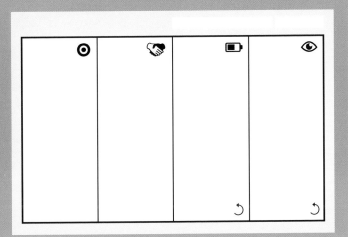

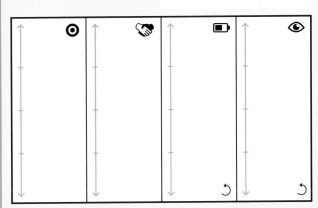

TAM – Planning Mode
Align together on the team mission and
the objectives to be achieved by whom and
how with the Team Alignment Map. Visually
reduce fears and risks for higher chances of
success. Use the TAM as a co-planning tool
to engage people from the start and to build
higher levels of buy-in and commitment (p.
86).

TAM – Assessment Mode
Don't let collaboration blind spots compromise your projects. TAM assessments are
fast and reveal the unseen in a visual and
neutral manner. Create genuine opportunities for productive dialogue, collective "aha"
moments that do not stigmatize those who
wish to speak up, and reinforce team learning behaviors (p. 104).

The Four Trust and Psychological Safety Add-Ons

Use the four add-ons to:

- Clarify the rules of the game with the Team Contract

- Ask good questions with the Fact Finder

- Demonstrate consideration for others with the Respect Card

- Manage conflict constructively with the Nonviolent Requests Guide

The Team Alignment Map and the Team Contract are co-creation tools. The Fact Finder, the Nonviolent Requests Guide, and the Respect Card are behavioral tools. They're used individually to improve everyday interactions.

Improves Activities ● ● ● ●
Improves Climate ● ● ● ● ●

Improve team climate

JOINT MISSION

Use the four trust add-ons to build a safer team climate

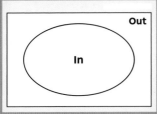

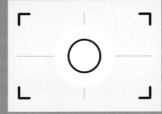

The Team Contract
Define team rules with the Team Contract. Address behaviors, values, decision-making, and communication, and frame expectations in terms of failure as a team. Create a transparent and fair environment that fosters team learning behaviors and harmony (see p. 184).

The Fact Finder
The Fact Finder proposes powerful questions that transform unproductive assumptions, judgments, limitations, and generalizations into observable facts and experiences. Inquire like a pro — restore clarity in discussions when you feel puzzled. Build more trust by demonstrating a genuine interest in what others are saying (see p. 204).

The Respect Card
The Respect Card suggests tips for being tactful and demonstrating consideration by (1) valuing others (2) demonstrating respect. This makes conversations less efficient from a task perspective but adds greatly to a safer team climate (see p. 220).

The Nonviolent Requests Guide
Don't make things worse by exploding emotionally; manage conflict constructively with the Nonviolent Requests Guide. Express legitimate negative feelings by using proper wording. Help others understand what's wrong and what should change in a nonaggressive manner and keep the team climate safe (see p. 236).

Common Challenges:
The Team Alignment
Map in Action

In Meetings

In Projects

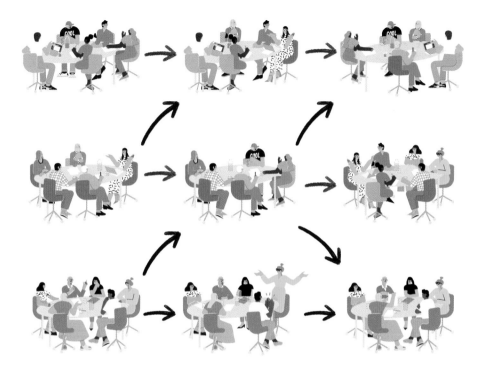

In Organizations

- Empower teams, p. 174
- Engage large groups, p. 176
- Facilitate collaboration across departments and functions, p. 178
- Negotiate and allocate resources, p. 180
- Integrate the TAM with strategy tools, p. 182
- Assess the readiness of strategic initiatives, p. 184

What to Read First

Leaders of Organizations

You will benefit from reading the Essentials (p. 1), learning to De-silo organizations (p. 168). You can lead better conversations in your teams by getting a firm understanding of

Entrepreneurs

You can start with the Essentials (p. 1) and learn how to use the TAM for Keeping projects on track (p. 140), and bring rules to a team by signing the Team Contract (p. 184).

Team Coaches

You should ensure that you know all about Aligning for successful team-work (p. 48) and understanding Are we still on track? (p. 140). Additionally, all of the add-on tools in

Project Leaders

You should thoroughly understand the <u>Essentials (p. 1)</u>, and learn how to use the TAM for <u>Keeping projects on track (p. 140)</u>. You can get rules in place on your team with the <u>the Team Contract (p. 184).</u>

Team Members

You can get a quick overview with <u>Essentials (p. 1)</u>. You can then learn to <u>Run move-to-action meetings (p. 126)</u>, and have better conversations with <u>the Fact Finder (p. 204)</u>.

Educators

You must understand the <u>Essentials (p. 1)</u> first. You will find <u>Aligning for successful team work (planning mode) (p. 86)</u>, and helping teams check: <u>Are we still on track? (p. 111)</u>.

Discover the Team Alignment Map

What it is and how it works

"Working together itself takes work."

Herbert Clark, Psycholinguist

Overview

__Understand__ the layout and content of each column, __plan__ and reduce risks, and __assess__ projects and teams.

1.1
Getting Started: The Four Pillars of the Team Alignment Map

How to describe joint objectives, team member commitments, required resources, and risks.

1.2
Planning Who Does What with the Team Alignment Map (Planning Mode)

Start with a forward pass (the plan), then make a backward pass (to lower any risks).

1.3
Keeping Team Members on Track (Assessment Mode)

Use the Team Alignment Map to assess team readiness or address ongoing problems.

1.1

Getting Started:
The Four Pillars of the
Team Alignment Map

How to describe joint objectives, team member
commitments, required resources, and risks.

The Workspace

The workspace is divided into two parts: the header area to frame the collaboration and the content area to guide meetings with regard to the four pillars. Each pillar covers a crucial aspect for any successful collaboration.

Joint Objectives
p. 54
What do we intend to achieve together, concretely?

Joint Commitments
p. 62
Who will do what?

Joint Resources
p. 70
What resources do we need?

Joint Risks
p. 78
What can prevent us from succeeding?

Dive Deeper
To discover the academic back-stage of the Team Alignment Map, please read p. 258: Mutual Understanding and Common Ground (in Psycholinguistics).

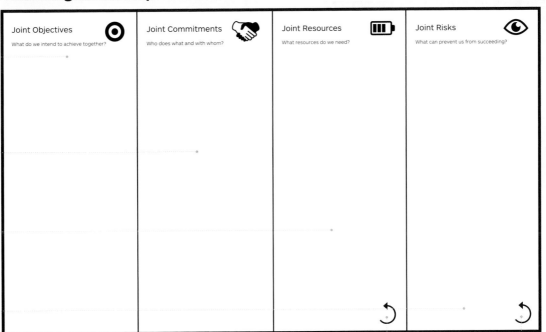

Header Area
Give context and focus.

Mission
Give meaning and context by explaining the purpose of the meeting or the project (p. 52–53).

Period
Set a timeframe in days, months, or a deadline to start getting real (p. 52–53).

Team Alignment Map

Mission:

Period:

Joint Objectives
What do we intend to achieve together?

Joint Commitments
Who does what and with whom?

Joint Resources
What resources do we need?

Joint Risks
What can prevent us from succeeding?

Content Area
Space to work.

⊕Strategyzer

Backward pass indicators
Visual reminders that risks must be addressed as a team (backward pass, p. 78–79).

Mission and Period

A mission is the starting point of any collaboration, the glue that brings everyone together. It helps everyone understand what's at stake and provides a rationale for personal engagement because:

- It is appealing, or
- Everyone feels concerned, or
- It is a necessary part of everyone's duties.

Participants constantly ask themselves "Why am I here?" when missions are unclear. Attention and participation drop, the conversation jumps from subject to subject, and dialogue becomes inconsistent, making participants feeling confused and often bored.

Periods set a time horizon for the team. Time limits are essential: they help remove exotic considerations in terms of goals and immerse everyone in the realm of concrete actions.

The header area helps participants simply understand why they are there and creates interest in listening and participating.

+
Describing Meaningful Missions

To benefit from higher levels of team buy-in and motivation, describe missions positively and from a participant's perspective. Respect these criteria as much as possible when writing down a mission: challenging, audacious, unique, unusual, or fun.

Example
- DO: Strengthen our profitability and secure our salaries for the next three years.
  [goal + benefit]
- DON'T: Reduce costs by 30%.

As described by Amy Edmondson, people must agree on and feel proud of their team's mission to motivate their personal efforts and overcome the relational and technical hurdles to succeed (Edmondson and Harvey 2017; Deci and Ryan 1985; Locke and Latham 1990).

Search keywords: mission statements; naming projects.

+
"Buy-In Check"

It's ideal for a mission to be validated using the following statement:

For the entire duration of the mission (M), every participant is able to give meaning to his or her personal contribution (X) by thinking:

"I am doing X because my group is doing M and requires my X, and that is meaningful for me."

Mission
What's the challenge?
What do we want to create
or improve?

Period
For how long?
Until when?

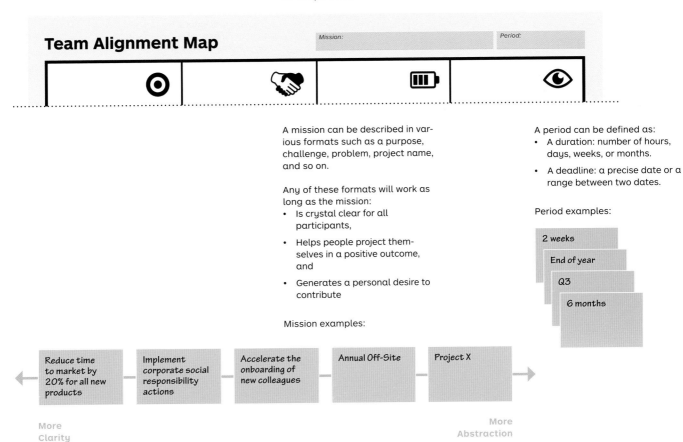

A mission can be described in various formats such as a purpose, challenge, problem, project name, and so on.

Any of these formats will work as long as the mission:
- Is crystal clear for all participants,
- Helps people project themselves in a positive outcome, and
- Generates a personal desire to contribute

Mission examples:

A period can be defined as:
- A duration: number of hours, days, weeks, or months.
- A deadline: a precise date or a range between two dates.

Period examples:

Joint Objectives

What do we intend to achieve together, concretely?

Team Alignment Map

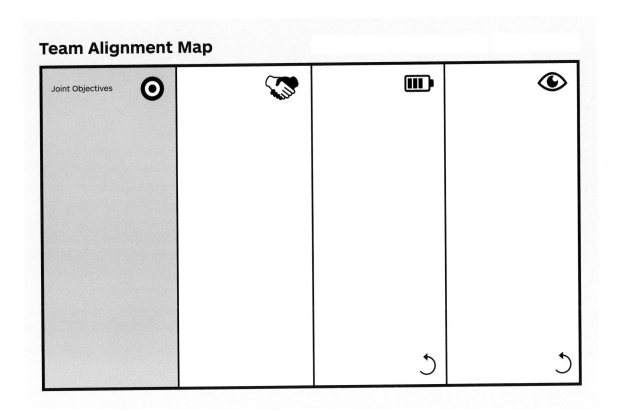

Joint Objectives

Does anyone understand what we're supposed to do?

What Are Joint Objectives?

Clear joint objectives align participants' intentions on what needs to get done, expressed in terms of:

- Goals (intention to be achieved)
- Objectives (measurable goals)
- Activities (something to be done)
- Actions (pieces of activities)
- Tasks (pieces of actions)
- Work packages (work given to a person)
- Results (consequences of activities)
- Deliverables (synonym for results)
- Outcomes (synonym for results)
- Products, services (synonyms for results)

The TAM is a semi-structured tool. The key here is to agree on actionable work; however, it may be shaped. A typical TAM contains 3–10 joint objectives. If you have more than 10 objectives, ask the team if the mission is not too broad or ambiguous. You may be describing several projects at once. Consider splitting it into several TAMs if this is the case.

Setting joint objectives as a team
helps break down the mission
into actionable pieces of work.

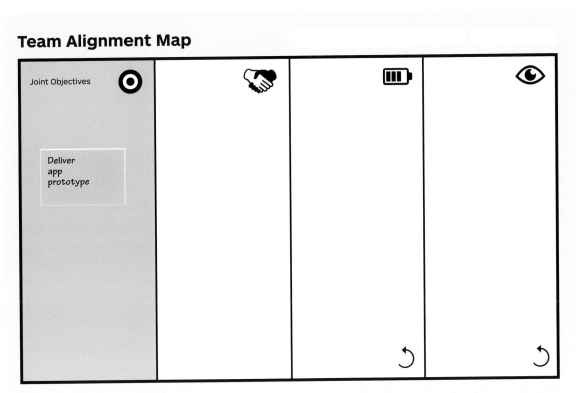

Team Alignment Map

Joint Objectives

Deliver
app
prototype

Ask
- What do we intend to achieve together, concretely?
- What do we have to do?
- What do we need to deliver?
- What work must be done?

Examples

| Create a plan | Hire a consultant | Amend contracts | Negotiate leasing | Update product backlog |
| Paint the interior | Grant access rights | Install electrical wires | Standardize onboarding process | |

Examples of Joint Objectives

Joint objectives can be described in more or less detail.
The tradeoff is between clarity and speed.

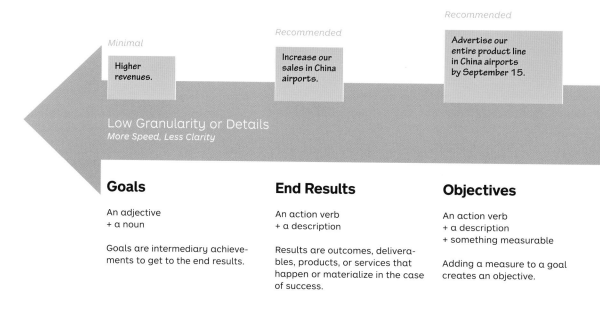

Minimal

Higher revenues.

Recommended

Increase our sales in China airports.

Recommended

Advertise our entire product line in China airports by September 15.

Low Granularity or Details
More Speed, Less Clarity

Goals

An adjective
+ a noun

Goals are intermediary achievements to get to the end results.

End Results

An action verb
+ a description

Results are outcomes, deliverables, products, or services that happen or materialize in the case of success.

Objectives

An action verb
+ a description
+ something measurable

Adding a measure to a goal creates an objective.

As a market developer, I need an advertising budget, so that I can promote our product line in China airports.

Grow market share in China.

Grow market share by 20%, in China airports, for the entire product line, by the end of this fiscal year.

High Granularity or Details

Less Speed, More Clarity

User Stories

As a < *role* >,
I want < *objectives* >,
so that < *reason* >.

User stories are a technique to describe user requirements in agile software development. This approach is increasingly adopted by other industries to describe objectives from a user perspective.

Search: user story

OKR (Objectives and Key Results)

Goal + key results

OKR is a system to describe joint objectives, initially developed by Andy Grove while he was CEO of Intel. The method became famous after being adopted by Google. To write an OKR you have to specify measurable key results for each goal.

Search: OKR

SMART Objectives

SMART stands for specific, measurable, achievable, realistic, and time-bound. This way of describing objectives is usually associated with the popular concept of "management by objectives" presented by Peter Drucker in the 1950s.

It's of great use in situations where objectives do not change on a regular basis.

Search: SMART Objectives

+

Always start your TAM by clarifying the joint objectives

Work can't be directed and organized as a team if the joint objectives are unclear. It was Thomas Shelling's (game theory pioneer and Nobel Prize winner) insight that "joint actions are created from the goal backward. Two people realize they have common goals, realize their actions are interdependent, and work backward to find a way of coordinating their actions in a joint action that will reach those goals." In other words, regardless of its duration (for example, 3 weeks, 3 months, or 3 years), a plan has no value in terms of work if the objectives are unclear.

+

Objectives decomposition and granularity

The Team Alignment Map has not been designed for detailed task decomposition and tracking. The tool helps members align rapidly on key topics to collaborate more effectively. If higher levels of granularity are required, report and decompose the joint objectives in a project management tool after the team alignment session. Validate the decomposed list with the team afterwards.

Search keywords: work breakdown structure; backlog

Joint Commitments

Who will do what?

Team Alignment Map

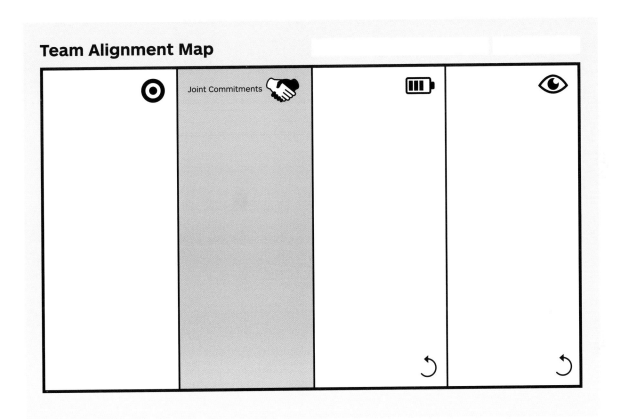

Joint Commitments

What Are Joint Commitments?

By establishing joint commitments, team members commit to take over and carry out one or more joint objectives. There is not much to write on the notes; names and high-level roles are usually enough. However, the ritual of each member committing in front of others plays an important role. This can be done in two ways:

- The team member writes his or her name next to the objectives he or she will be responsible for, or,
- The team member agrees by saying "okay," "I agree," "fine for me," or "I'll do it" if someone has placed their name on the TAM.

Ambiguous commitments result in a lack of accountability and occur mostly in teams where commitments are implicit, i.e. unspoken. Unspoken commitments create a gray zone in which participants can presuppose what the others will do at their convenience, which increases the likelihood of confusion and conflict. This can be reduced just by speaking clearly.

The Joint Commitment Ritual: Discover the Work of Margaret Gilbert

Margaret Gilbert is a British philosopher who investigated the notion of joint commitment for decades. She observed that to create pertinent joint commitments it is necessary and sufficient that team members express their readiness to be committed in front of others (Gilbert 2014). This makes commitments enter the team's common ground or common knowledge (see Dive Deeper, p. 252). Agreeing openly on joint commitments creates moral obligations and rights. Each team member who makes a commitment has the moral obligation to do his or her part, and in return the right to expect others to do their part. These rights and obligations bind team members and act as a powerful driving force.

Search: Margaret Gilbert philosophy

Joint commitments move participants
from the status of individual to the
status of active team member.

Team Alignment Map

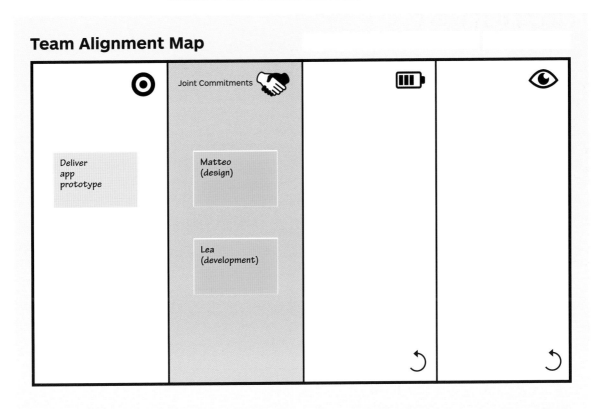

Ask
- **Who will do what?**
- Who commits to what?
- How will we work together?
- What's everyone's role?

Joint commitments are
usually placed to the right of
the related joint objective.

Examples of Joint Commitments

Joint commitments can vary from a name to a name with a list of high-level tasks. What matters is that everyone understands who will do what and agrees.

Temporary

Minimal

All

Finance

IT

SJ

Lea

Yann + Nigel + Eve

Low Granularity or Details
More Speed, Less Clarity

[Team] or [Department]

A team's name is useful when not all commitments can be clarified right away. This is the quickest method, but commitments will need to be clarified rapidly to avoid misunderstandings.

[Initials] or [Names]

Initials and first names are fast and useful for team members who are used to working together.

Lea
(development)

Matteo
(design)
Lea
(development)

Matteo:
- Create paper version
- Design digital assets

Lea:
- Technical architecture
- Code and test

High Granularity or Details

Less Speed, More Clarity

[Name] + [Role]

In addition to the name, describing each person's role or task concisely increases mutual clarity, while not slowing down the alignment session.

[Name] + [Main Tasks/Responsibilities]

High-level tasks can also be added. This longer approach is sometimes used by newly created teams. Beware of assigning subtasks that meet an objective in the Joint Objectives column to avoid confusing the team about what goes in each column.

Joint Resources

What resources do we need?

Team Alignment Map

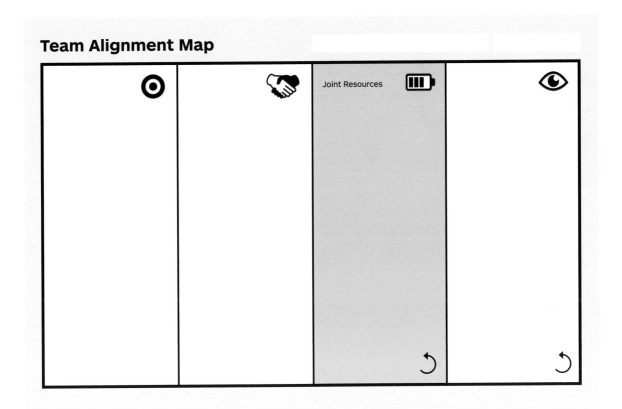

Joint Resources

What Are Joint Resources?

All human activities require resources such as time, capital, or equipment. Describing the joint resources consists of estimating these requirements so that every team member can contribute successfully. This anchors the team in the real world by increasing the joint awareness of what is eventually needed to achieve the mission.

When resources are lacking, teams lose the ability to deliver because individuals get stuck. Workflows are interrupted and the proper achievement of the mission is compromised. Estimating and negotiating resources is key but insufficient. Resources must then be allocated, i.e. be made available for team members to perform. Do not hesitate to insist on this point in case of doubt.

+
Resource status

The status of a resource can be indicated as follows:

Available

Matteo
10 days ✓

Not available

Lea
12 days ✗

Don't know

Sam
12 days ?

Joint resources help the team evaluate
what is needed by each team member
to do his or her part.

Team Alignment Map

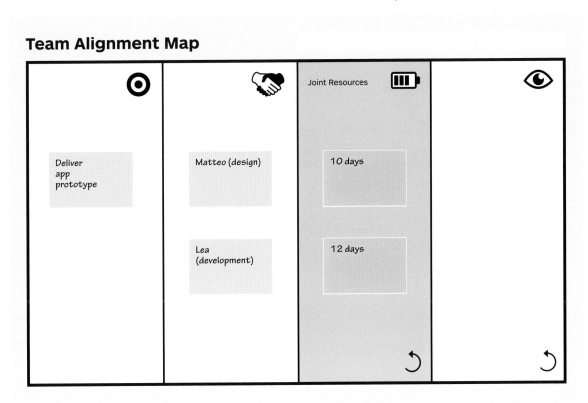

Ask

- **What resources do we need?**
- What should be made available or acquired?
- What is missing for everyone to contribute successfully?
- What are the necessary means to achieve our work?

Examples

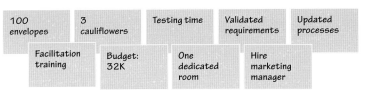

Examples of Joint Resources

If a team member needs something to do his or her work, then it's a resource! Resource needs can be described with more or less accuracy; the tradeoff is always between speed and clarity.

Minimal

Pablo

Office in China

Accurate data

Low Granularity or Details
More Speed, Less Clarity

[Resource]

Designating the resources can be a first step. That keeps the conversation moving in the right direction, i.e. identifying what is needed to get the job done.

Recommended

Pablo – 10 days

Flyers – 100

Travel budget $20K

With constraints

Need Pablo for 10 days at a max. cost of $1.5K/day

Print 100 flyers (needed before June 3rd)

Validate $20K travel budget before the end of the week.

High Granularity or Details
Less Speed, More Clarity

☐ People: such as staffing, working hours, skills (technical, social), training, motivation

☐ Equipment and tools: such as office desks, meeting rooms, furniture, vehicles, machines

☐ Financial: such as budgets, cash, credit

☐ Materials: such as raw materials, supplies

☐ Technology: such as applications, computers, online services, network infrastructure needs

☐ Information: such as documents, data, access rights

☐ Legal: such as copyrights, patents, permits, contracts

☐ Organizational: such as processes, internal support, decisions

[Resource] + [Estimated Quantity]

Naming and quantifying the resources creates a superior level of alignment and realism among team members. Suggest an interval or amount (1–10; $20–80K) when it's difficult to provide a single estimate.

[Verb] + [Estimated Quantity] + [Resource] + [Constraint]

This longer template can help align the team when high levels of accuracy are needed for critical resources. Used only in specific cases.

Joint Risks

What can prevent us from succeeding?

Team Alignment Map

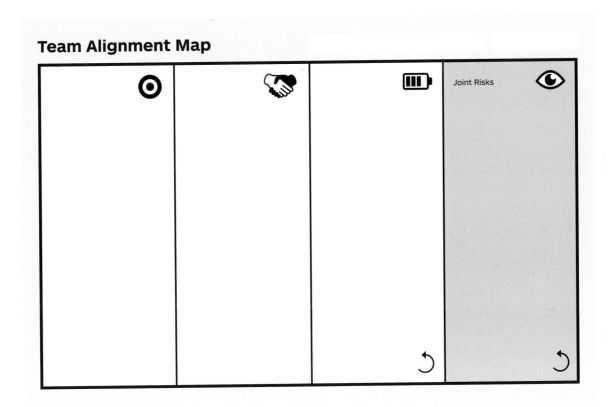

Joint Risks

I told you we were going too fast.

What Are Joint Risks?

Risk-free projects deliver... nothing. All projects carry risks related to their inherent degree of uncertainty. Risks are events that, if they occur, create unwanted obstacles. These obstacles make it more difficult for the team to achieve the mission. They can negatively impact the costs, the deadlines or quality of the deliverables, and even damage personal relationships. In the worst-case scenario, a risk that occurs can cause the entire project and team to fail.

The Team Alignment Map helps reduce project risk in three main steps:

1. Risk identification
   By filling in the joint risks column

2. Risk analysis
   By discussing the risk exposure of each entry

3. Risk mitigation
   By performing a backward pass
   (please read p. 88–89)

Risk management discussions matter: they increase the team's resilience — hence the likelihood of achieving the mission successfully.

+
Risk exposure

An easy technique is to mark risk exposure with a score or letter somewhere in the note.

For example: H = High, M = Medium, L = Low

(risk exposure = risk likelihood x risk impact)

+
Professional risk management

The TAM is designed for on-the-fly rapid risk management; it is not a substitute for in-depth risk analysis and management tools. Please refer to professional techniques in that case.

Search keywords: risk management, risk management process, risk management tools.

Joint risks help the team anticipate and fix potential problems proactively.

Team Alignment Map

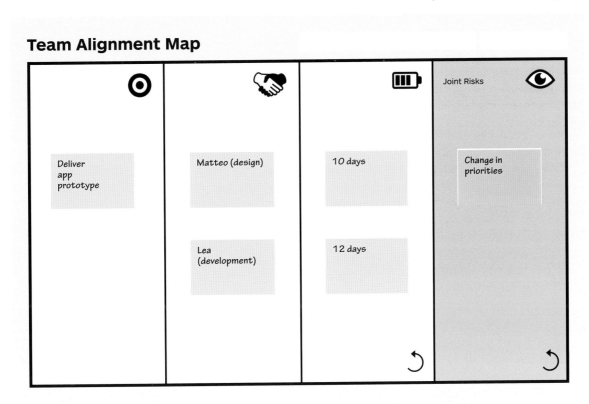

Ask

- **What can prevent us from succeeding?**
- What might go wrong?
- What's our worst-case scenario?
- What are problems/threats/dangers/ side effects in achieving our objectives?
- Are there any particular fears/objections?
- What would make us consider a plan B?

Examples

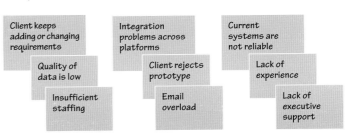

Examples of Joint Risks

When describing risks, pragmatism should prevail.

At one extreme, so many things can possibly go wrong that a team can spend more time describing risks accurately than working to achieve the mission. At the other extreme, overoptimism, doing nothing in terms of risk identification, may cause the project to fail for easily avoidable reasons. A compromise is to describe risks succinctly, and detail only those with the highest risk exposure.

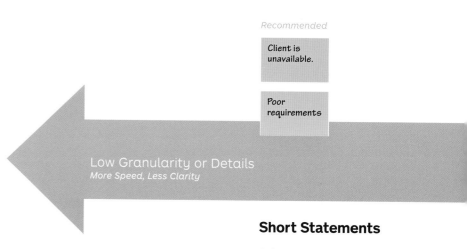

Recommended

Client is unavailable.

Poor requirements

Low Granularity or Details
More Speed, Less Clarity

Short Statements

A short statement is better than no risk identification at all. This is the spirit of assessing risks with the Team Alignment Map.

With consequence

Client unavailability may cause severe delays.

Poor initial requirements may result in servers' downtime.

Detailed

Client unavailability caused by the time difference may result in a 6–12-month delay and a 40% increase in costs.

Poor initial requirements caused by systems engineers being overloaded may result in misconfigured servers and 30–60% downtime.

There is a risk that the client is not available because she lives in a different time zone, which could result in a 6–12-month delay and a 40% increase in costs.

There is a risk that we get poor initial requirements because systems engineers are overloaded, which could result in misconfigured servers and 30–60% downtime.

High Granularity or Details
Less Speed, More Clarity

[Risk] may [Consequence]

[Event] caused by [Cause/s] may result in [Quantifiable consequence/s on joint objectives]

There is risk that [Event] because [Cause/s], which could result in [Quantifiable consequence/s on joint objectives]

+
Risks checklist

☐ Internal: such as risks caused by the team itself, mistakes, defects, lack of preparation, lack of skills, quality of deliverables, miscommunication, staffing, roles, conflict, etc.

☐ Equipment: such as risks caused by technical problems, products and services used by the team, insufficient quality of tools, building, etc.

☐ Organizational: such as risks caused by management and other teams in the same organization, lack of support, politics, logistics, funding, etc.

☐ External: such as risks caused by clients, end users, suppliers, regulatory problems, financial markets, weather conditions, etc.

+
The templates on the right are more formal and describe risks in much more detail. They do, however, significantly increase the effort of alignment. To avoid discouraging the team, favor short statements such as presented on the left and use these detailed templates as additional guides for the discussion. If necessary, switch to professional risk management tools.

1.2
Planning Who Does What with the Team Alignment Map (Planning Mode)

Start with a forward pass to create the plan,
then make a backward pass to lower any risks.

Forward and Backward Pass

Planning with the Team Alignment Map is a two-step process.

1,2,3,4,5
The Forward Pass

6,7
The Backward Pass

The first part of the process, called the forward pass, consists of planning together. Participants describe what is needed to collaborate effectively by filling in each column in a logical order from left to right. This sets a big picture, both in terms of expectations and problems, on which participants can reflect to increase their chances of success.

The forward pass starts bringing everyone together as a real team. Team members jointly consider each other's contributions and needs, and common understanding develops.

The second part is called the backward pass and is aimed at reducing the level of execution risk. Practically speaking, this part consists of removing as much content as possible from the last two columns. This happens by creating, adapting, and removing content from the rest of the map. In other words, latent problems, such as missing resources and open risks, are transformed into new objectives and new commitments.

Fixing and removing problems visually, together, gives a sense of progression. Motivation and engagement increase as participants see that the risks they described disappear because they are properly addressed. This also allows confirmation of the mission and the period, at the very end of the backward pass.

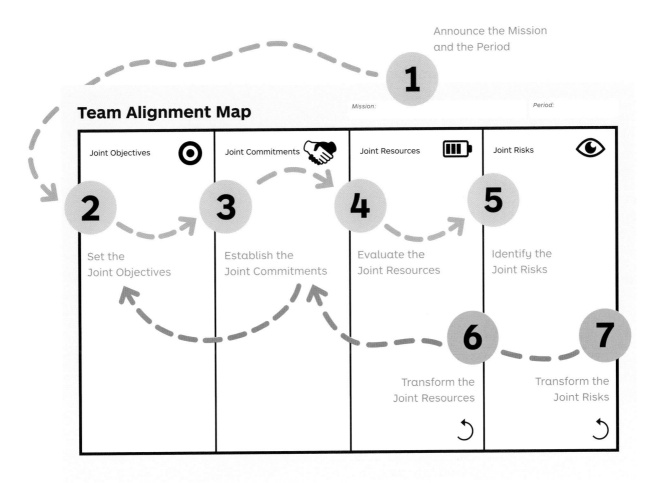

Team Alignment Map

Announce the Mission and the Period
1

Mission: Period:

Joint Objectives ◎	Joint Commitments 🤝	Joint Resources 🔋	Joint Risks 👁

2   **3**   **4**   **5**

Set the
Joint Objectives

Establish the
Joint Commitments

Evaluate the
Joint Resources

Identify the
Joint Risks

6   **7**

Transform the
Joint Resources

Transform the
Joint Risks

↺   ↺

Example at Work

The Forward Pass
Develop a Social Media Strategy

Honora, Pablo, Matteo, Tess, and Lou work for a communications agency. Their mission is to develop a social media strategy for an important client in record time. They decide to align with the Team Alignment Map and here is the result of the forward and the backward pass.

1

Announce the Mission and the Period

Develop Social Media Strategy

4 Weeks

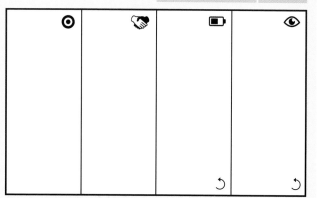

2

Set the Joint Objectives

Develop Social Media Strategy

4 Weeks

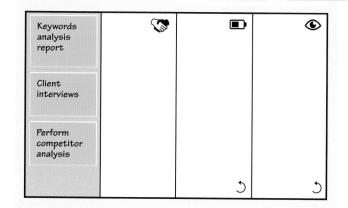

Keywords analysis report

Client interviews

Perform competitor analysis

4
Evaluate the Joint Resources

Develop Social Media Strategy | 4 Weeks

Keywords analysis report	Honora: *analyze* Matteo: *write*	Analytics software	👁
Client interviews	All	Missing database access	
Perform competitor analysis	Pablo, Tess, Lou	Tess lacks time	
		↺	↺

3
Establish the Joint Commitments

Develop Social Media Strategy | 4 Weeks

Keywords analysis report	Honora: *analyze* Matteo: *write*	🔋	👁
Client interviews	All		
Perform competitor analysis	Pablo, Tess, Lou		
		↺	↺

5
Identify the Joint Risks

Develop Social Media Strategy | 4 Weeks

Keywords analysis report	Honora: *analyze* Matteo: *write*	Analytics software	Client is not available
Client interviews	All	Missing database access	Overreliance on data
Perform competitor analysis	Pablo, Tess, Lou	Tess lacks time	
		↺	↺

Example at Work

The Backward Pass
Develop a Social Media Strategy

6
Transform the Joint Resources

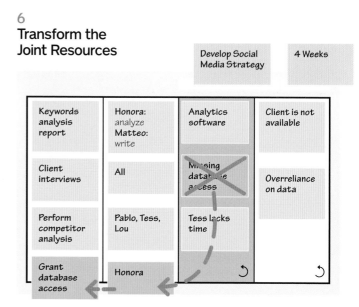

- Analytics software: The analytics software is available, the note is checked, and there's nothing special to do.
- Missing database access: Honora knows how to grant database access to the team, so she creates a new objective and a new commitment. The missing resource is removed from the column.
- Tess lacks time: A solution must still be found, so the element remains in this column.

7
Transform the Joint Risks

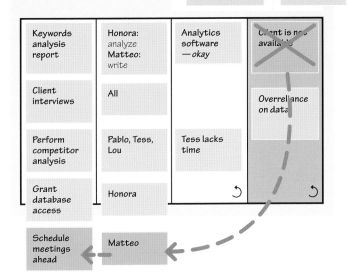

- Client is not available: There is a risk that the client is not available for the interviews, so Matteo commits to scheduling all meetings ahead of time. The risk is removed from the column.
- Overreliance on data: Nothing really can be done here except to keep that risk in mind. The team agrees to leave that risk as a reminder.

Team Validation

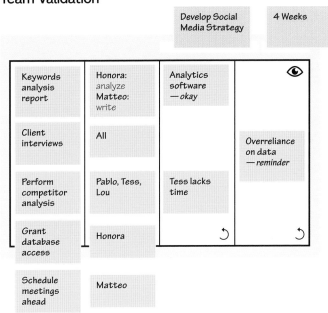

- The team agrees that work can start.
- A solution still needs to be found to free up time for Tess.
- Everyone knows it, which makes a big difference for her.

Example at Home

The Forward Pass
Successful Move to Geneva

Angela works for an international organization and she has just been relocated to its headquarters in Geneva, Switzerland. Together with her husband, Giuseppe, and their children, Renato, Manu, and Lydia, they decide to align to ensure a successful move. Here is what they discuss during the forward and the backward passes.

1
Announce the Mission and the Period

🎯	🤝	🔋	👁
			↵ ↵

Successful move to Geneva

3 months

2
Set the Joint Objectives

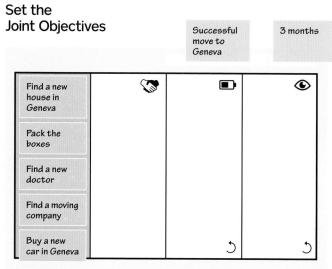

	🤝	🔋	👁
Find a new house in Geneva			
Pack the boxes			
Find a new doctor			
Find a moving company			
Buy a new car in Geneva		↵	↵

Successful move to Geneva

3 months

4
Evaluate the Joint Resources

Successful move to Geneva

3 months

Find a new house in Geneva	Angela	Need 50 packing boxes	👁
Pack the boxes	Renato, Manu, Lydia	$10K budget for the moving company	
Find a new doctor	Angela	$30K budget new car	
Find a moving company	Giuseppe	$5K budget for real estate agent	↺
Buy a new car in Geneva	Giuseppe		

3
Establish the Joint Commitments

Successful move to Geneva

3 months

Find a new house in Geneva	Angela	🔋	👁
Pack the boxes	Renato, Manu, Lydia		
Find a new doctor	Angela		
Find a moving company	Giuseppe		
Buy a new car in Geneva	Giuseppe	↺	↺

5
Identify the Joint Risks

Successful move to Geneva

3 months

Find a new house in Geneva	Angela	Need 50 packing boxes	👁
Pack the boxes	Renato, Manu, Lydia	$10K budget for the moving company	Furniture might be damaged during the move
Find a new doctor	Angela	$30K budget new car	Might need temporary storage space in Geneva
Find a moving company	Giuseppe	$5K budget for real estate agent	↺
Buy a new car in Geneva	Giuseppe		

Example at Home

The Backward Pass
Successful Move to Geneva

6
Transform the Joint Resources

			Successful move to Geneva	3 months

- Need 50 packing boxes: Angela will order the boxes today.
- $45K total budget (for the moving company, new car, real estate agent): Giuseppe will ensure that the money is available in the current bank account.

7
Transform the Joint Risks

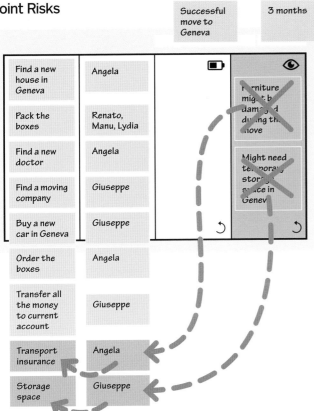

- Furniture might be damaged during transportation: Angela will take out transport insurance with their usual insurance company.
- Might need temporary storage space in Geneva: Giuseppe will contact the HR department for a recommendation and ensure that sufficient storage space is available.

Team Validation

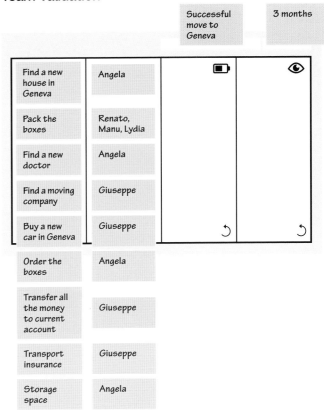

- Everyone agrees and gets to work to make a successful move.

Example with Friends

The Forward Pass
A Great Birthday Party

Louise's birthday is approaching, and her parents, Mathilde and Bernard, want to organize a beautiful party. Her best friend, Thomas, also wants to help. Here is how they teamed up to do a forward and a backward pass.

1
Announce the Mission and the Period

Great Birthday Party	2 weeks

🎯	🤝	🔋	👁
		↺	↺

2
Set the Joint Objectives

Great Birthday Party	2 weeks

	🤝	🔋	👁
Create guestlist			
Send the invitations			
Decorate the house			
Prepare the cakes and buy drinks		↺	↺

Evaluate the Joint Resources

Great Birthday Party	2 weeks		

Create guestlist	Louise	🔋	👁
Send the invitations	Mathilde	20 envelopes	
Decorate the house	Bernard	100 balloons	
Prepare the cakes and buy drinks	Thomas	Sugar, chocolate, and butter	↺

Establish the Joint Commitments

Great Birthday Party	2 weeks

Create guestlist	Louise	🔋	👁
Send the invitations	Mathilde		
Decorate the house	Bernard		
Prepare the cakes and buy drinks	Thomas	↺	↺

Identify the Joint Risks

Great Birthday Party	2 weeks

Create guestlist	Louise	🔋	👁
Send the invitations	Mathilde	20 envelopes	Children might be afraid of the dog
Decorate the house	Bernard	100 balloons	Noise complaint from Ms. Picky (our neighbor)
Prepare the cakes and buy drinks	Thomas	Sugar, chocolate, and butter	↺

Example with Friends

The Backward Pass
A Great Birthday Party

6
Transform the Joint Resources

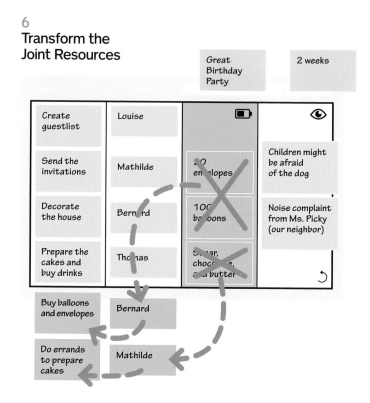

- 20 envelopes and 100 balloons:
  Bernard will take care of this.
- Sugar, chocolate, and butter:
  Mathilde must go to the pharmacy
  and she will stop on the way back to buy
  the ingredients.

7
Transform the Joint Risks

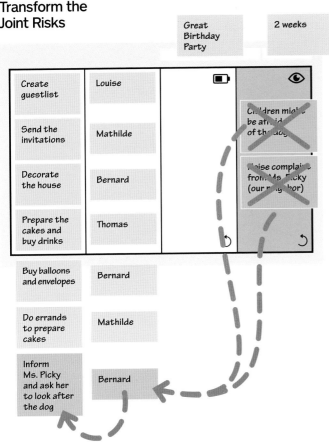

- Children might be afraid of the dog and Ms. Picky might complain about the noise: Bernard will inform Mrs. Picky immediately and ask her to keep the dog the afternoon of the party.

Team Validation

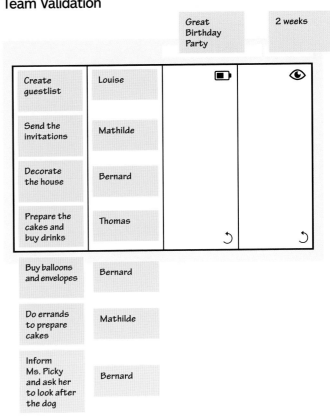

- Everyone agrees and they start preparing a great birthday party.

Pro Tips

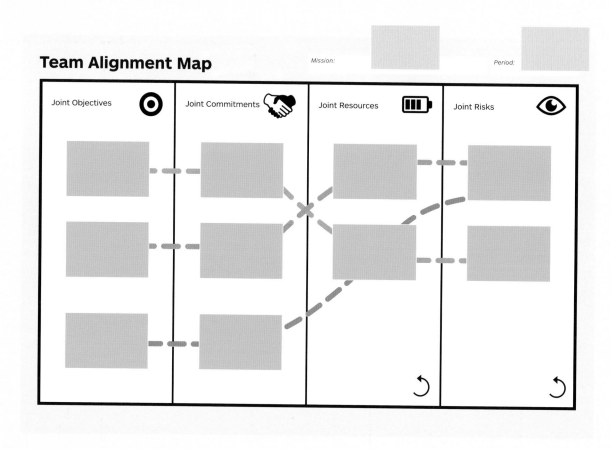

Visualizing Relationships
Simply draw lines to visualize relationships.

Removed Items

What to do with the joint risks and joint resources removed during the backward pass?

Option 1
On the left: in front of the new objectives

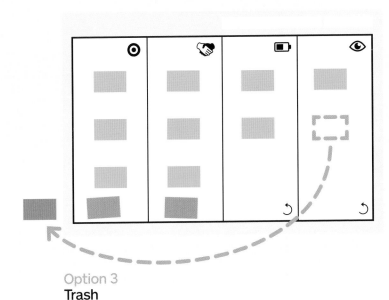

Option 2
On the right on the wall

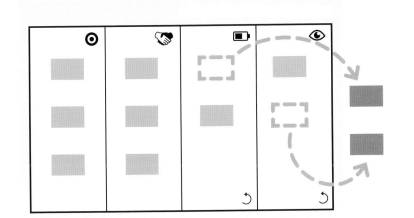

Option 3
Trash

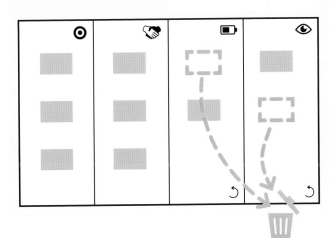

1.3
Keeping Team Members on Track (Assessment Mode)

Use the Team Alignment Map to assess team readiness or address ongoing problems.

How to Use the Team Alignment Map to Assess Projects and Teams

The Team Alignment Map can easily turn into an alert system that reveals blind spots and prevents the accumulation of small perception gaps from becoming big problems.

Rapid visual assessments with the TAM can help the team ensure that minimal success requirements are met:
- Initially, to have a good project start.
- Later on, to remain on the right track.

Too often we embark on projects where these minimal requirements are not met and collaborating turns into permanent crisis management. This happens when the team lacks preparation or when there are collaboration blind spots, i.e. when someone thinks he or she knows what others are thinking but is off base. Ensuring enough alignment from start to finish is essential to success, and with a rapid assessment the team can visualize the level of alignment and act early enough to avoid preventable problems.

Assessing consists of asking every team member if they think they can do their part successfully. This is done with a vote that can be anonymous if necessary. The image resulting from a vote is neutral, and is then interpreted as a team; repair actions are undertaken if the alignment is insufficient.

To start assessing, draw four horizontal sliders in each column and add the following values to each slider (starting from the bottom of the map) as illustrated in the figure on the next page:
1. Joint objectives: unclear, neutral, clear
2. Joint commitments: implicit, neutral, explicit
3. Joint resources: missing, neutral, available
4. Joint risks: underestimated, neutral, under control

Then follow by applying this basic three-step process:

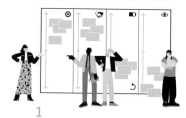

1
Reveal
Participants vote individually and acknowledge the result collectively.

2
Reflect
Problem areas are identified and analyzed as a team.

3
Repair
Decisions are made to fix the problems and are validated together.

Team Alignment Map

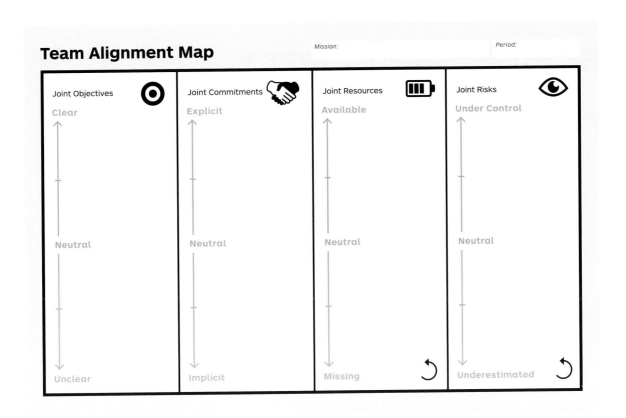

Joint Objectives	Joint Commitments	Joint Resources	Joint Risks
Clear	Explicit	Available	Under Control
Neutral	Neutral	Neutral	Neutral
Unclear	Implicit	Missing	Underestimated

Step 1: Reveal

Team members vote to reveal whether they believe they can contribute successfully.

1
Announce the topic
What's the challenge?

Teresa   Luca   Jeremy   Mara

2
Vote individually
Do you think you can do your part?

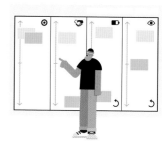

Teresa thinks:

- Joint objectives: what we intend to achieve together is clear.
- Joint commitments: we have explicitly discussed each one of our role and commitments.
- Joint resources: we have the resources we need to do our jobs.
- Joint risks: the risks we face are under control.

Luca thinks:

- Joint objectives: what we intend to achieve together is clear.
- Joint commitments: our roles are implicit; mutual commitments have not been discussed.
- Joint resources: we miss critical resources to do our jobs.
- Joint risks: some risks are under control and some are underestimated.

Mara thinks:

- Joint objectives: some objectives are clear and some are not.
- Joint commitments: some commitments have been discussed and some are implicit.
- Joint resources: some resources are available but are not sufficient to do our jobs.
- Joint risks: some risks are under control and some are underestimated.

Jeremy thinks:

- Joint objectives: what we intend to achieve together is unclear; I'm confused.
- Joint commitments: our roles are implicit; mutual commitments have not been discussed.
- Joint resources: we miss critical resources to do our jobs.
- Joint risks: the risks we face are underestimated.

3
Acknowledge the result
What's the collective result?

The "aha" moment. The display of the vote triggers group awareness and problem recognition.

Step 2: Reflect

Identify perception gaps and discuss to understand the causes.

The vertical distribution of votes helps the team understand whether each member is in a position to contribute successfully and the level of alignment in the team, i.e. if team members share the same perception.

The ideal vote occurs when all votes are in the green zone. When a participant enters his or her entire vote into the green zone, he or she reports that:

1. Objectives are clear
2. Commitments have been explicitly agreed
3. Resources are available to do his or her work
4. Risks are under control

In other words, a vote in the green zone indicates that the minimum requirements are met for a successful personal contribution. When the whole team votes in the same way, team members are positively aligned and the team is likely on the path to success because everyone thinks they can successfully contribute.

The team can also be negatively aligned, when the majority of votes are concentrated at the bottom of the red zone. This means that all team members express that they

4

Interpret the vote
Surprised or not surprised?
Is it more positive or negative for us?
Where are the problems?

cannot contribute at all. Any other voting pattern in the red zone signals a problem for one or more members, that something is unclear or missing and that should be addressed rapidly.

To summarize, the vertical position of votes shows whether a requirement is met or not; the higher the position the better. A concentration of votes illustrates alignment in the team, whereas dispersion indicates misalignment. The more votes are concentrated at the top, in the green zone, the higher the chances of success. The more votes are dispersed or concentrated at the bottom, in the red zone, the more problems are likely to appear while working together. In this case, better stop, talk, and take repair actions before it's too late.

Green zone

Higher likelihood of success

(all votes in the top third of the map)

It's okay when the majority of votes is in the green zone. The team is aligned and everyone is ready to perform. No need to discuss further; it's time to get back to work.

Red zone

Lower likelihood of success

(one or more votes in the bottom two-thirds of the sliders)

Problems are imminent when one or more votes are in the red zone. The requirements for a successful collaboration are not met for one or more team members. Better discuss to understand where the problems are and how to fix them before it's too late.

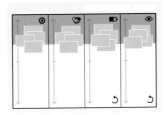

Example 1: Go ahead

This is the ideal vote. The team is positively aligned and confident that everyone can contribute successfully.

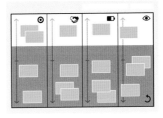

Example 2: Stop and talk

The four variables must be discussed and clarified. Some team members think that some requirements are okay (votes at the top), others that nothing is okay (votes at the bottom). This dispersion illustrates the highest level of misalignment.

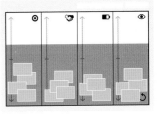

Example 3: Stop and talk

The four variables must be discussed. The team is negatively aligned: all members believe that nothing is okay.

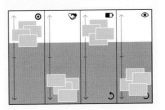

Example 4: Stop and talk

The team needs to discuss why commitments and risks are so low. For all team members, the joint commitments are unclear and joint risks are underestimated. Joint objectives appear clear and resources are available for the whole team.

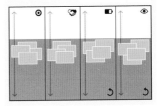

Example 5: Stop and talk

The four variables must be urgently discussed. All team members vote neutral. This is a typical vote for nonpriority projects or when participants are disengaged or prefer not to speak up.

Example 6: Stop and talk

The last two variables must be discussed. Joint objectives and joint commitments are clear, but there is a critical lack of resources and risks are somehow underestimated. This is a typical vote for teams in startups. The last two variables must be discussed.

5
Analyze the problems

What's causing the problems?
What causes the perception gaps?
What prevents that requirement from being
in the green zone?

The objective of this step is to discuss the
votes in the red zone and what causes
the perception gaps—the trigger questions
on the next page might help.

Discussion time may vary depending
on the situation. For example, a problem
with a missing resource, such as a software developer claiming three additional
days of work, is quite simple to understand.
Problems regarding unclear objectives,
implicit commitments, or risks will need
more time to be understood.

Trigger questions to analyze problems

These questions help spark collective thinking and dive deeper into possible issues. The following rule of thumb helps facilitate the analysis:

1. Ask a question
2. Listen to the answers
3. Summarize and share to validate understanding

High-level questions

What's your feeling about this vote?
What do you think is the problem?

Inquire deeper

Joint Objectives

- What are we supposed to achieve together, concretely?
- What will make our project a success?
- What are we supposed to deliver?
- What will the end result look like?
- What challenges do we have to address?
- What's the plan?

Joint Commitments

- Who will do what? With whom? For whom?
- What's everyone's role and responsibilities?
- What do we expect from each other, precisely?

Joint Resources

- What resources do we need?
- What is missing for everyone to do his or her part?

Joint Risks

- What can prevent us from succeeding?
- What's our worst-case scenario?
- What's our plan B?

Step 3: Repair

Repairing means taking concrete actions to ensure that the votes in the red zone are moved to the green zone in the next vote.

What causes problems is understood and it's time to redress the situation. Further explanations must be provided or decisions must be made. The resulting repair actions can vary considerably:

- Clarify or adapt something (mission, period, and the content of the four columns).
- Remove or add new content on the map.
- Make decisions outside the TAM, shift priorities, split the project into two or three projects, and so on.

As shown in 7, a final vote is conducted to validate the impact of the repair actions and to see if any problems remain. The assessment has been successful if the majority of votes is now in the green zone.

6

Decide and announce the repair actions
What concrete actions/measures should we take to redress the situation?
What can be done to get most of the votes in the green zone next time?

More questions for making decisions and acting

- So now what? What should we do, concretely?
- What actions must we take now? What's the priority?
- Where do we go from here? What do we decide?
- What are the immediate next steps?

+
Fixing the mission and period

- Clarify the mission
- Reframe the mission
- Review the scope
- Extend the period

+
Fixing the four variables

- Clarify
- Add
- Remove
- Adapt

+
Fixing outside the TAM

- Change priorities
- Split the project into sub-projects
- Assign to a different team, etc.

7
Team Validation
Do you think you can do your part now?

The new votes are in the green zone: great job! The situation is corrected, and everyone can get back to work.

Should some votes remain in the red zone: unfortunately, some problems still remain. In this case pragmatism prevails: the team and/or the team lead decide whether to resume an analysis cycle or move forward.

When to Assess

There are two types of assessments: when the project is kicked off (more frequent) and after (less frequent). The need for alignment is greatest at the beginning of projects and decreases over time as team members accumulate common ground (see Dive Deeper, p. 252). But changes in context and information can create dangerous blind spots that can be addressed by making rapid ad hoc validations.

Readiness assessments **"Are we having a good start?"**	Troubleshooting assessments **"Are we still on track?"**
What?	
• Are we ready to perform? • Will every member deliver optimally? • Shall we go or do we need to prepare more? • What are our chances of success?	• Can every member still deliver optimally? • Have any changes created harmful blind spots? • Are we still on the path to success?
When?	
• Weekly coordination meetings (10 minutes before the end of the meeting) • Project initiation meetings (at the beginning or the middle of the meeting)	• Project execution meetings (10 minutes before the end of the meeting) • On-demand meetings (at the beginning of the meeting)
How many?	
More frequent (until the actual kickoff) • Daily • Weekly • On-demand	Less frequent (after the actual kickoff) • Monthly • Quarterly • Every semester • On-demand

<u>Case study</u>
Healthcare company
500 employees

Will We Deliver on Time?

Simone is the regional boss of a mid-sized healthcare company. Her project managers manage five projects on average and complain about their work overload. Rumors are flying around that the customer relationship management (CRM) project, which ranks high in terms of business priorities, will not be delivering on time. Is there anything Simone should worry about?

1
Reveal

Simone organizes an on-demand troubleshooting assessment to understand whether the project will be delivered on time or not. The team of four is invited and they vote. Results illustrate that there is a problem with joint resources. All team members agree that there are not enough resources to complete the work as expected.

Adapted from S. Mastrogiacomo, S. Missonier, and R. Bonazzi, "Talk Before It's Too Late: Reconsidering the Role of Conversation in Information Systems Project Management." Journal of Management Information Systems *31, no. 1 (2014): 47–78.*

2
Reflect

The team reflects: members report high work overloads, which results in a persistent lack of time to complete all their tasks and their inability to maintain the deadline. Further investigation leads Simone to realize that some members are working on nonpriority tasks, out of the scope of this project, and beyond their responsibility.

There have been recent changes in the organization and somehow, this information didn't make it to this team. This is the turning point of the meeting: team members realize that they were unaware of these changes.

3
Repair

Simone explains that some activities are no longer to be performed by the team, since they will be externalized soon. She clarifies the new priorities and the objectives of the CRM project to the team. Team members are relieved and confirm with a new vote that under these new conditions everyone will be able to perform their parts on time.

The CRM project is eventually delivered on time.

Run Your First Assessment

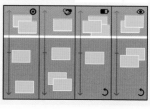

1
Reveal

2
Reflect

Announce the mission, project, or subject
- What's the challenge?

Vote individually
- Do you think you can do your part?

Acknowledge the result
- What's the collective result?

Interpret the vote
- Surprised or not surprised? Is it more positive or negative for us?
- Where are the problems?

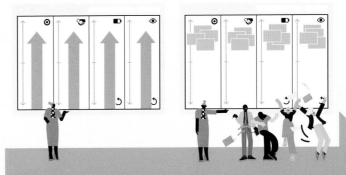

3 Repair

Analyze the problems

- What's causing the problems?
- What causes the perception gaps?
- What prevents that requirement from being in the green zone?

Decide and announce the repair actions

- What concrete actions/measures should we take to redress the situation?
- What can be done to get most of the votes in the green zone next time?

Team validation

- Do you think you can do your part now?

Put the Map into Action

How to use the Team Alignment Map

"Information is a
difference that makes
a difference."

Gregory Bateson, Anthropologist

Overview

Starting with successful meetings as building blocks, learn techniques to apply the Team Alignment Map in <u>meetings</u>, in <u>projects</u> (add time), and in <u>organizations</u> (add time and teams).

2.1
The Team Alignment Map
for Meetings

Run more productive, move-to-action meetings.

2.2
The Team Alignment Map
for Projects

Lower project risk and reduce execution problems.

2.3
The Team Alignment Map
for Organizational Alignment

Get alignment between leaders, teams, and
departments to break down internal silos.

2.1
The Team Alignment Map for Meetings

Run more productive, move-to-action meetings.

Shall we have another meeting?

Techniques to Run More Productive, Move-to-Action Meetings

Escape from conversations going around in endless loops. Use the TAM in your meetings to propel people from conversation to action, focus the team, and help everyone take action.

✓

Recommended for taking action

Use the TAM to help the participants move to action, coordinate, and deliver as a team.

×

Not recommended for exploring

Do not use the TAM to brainstorm or debate. The tool has not been designed to support exploratory discussions.

Focus the team
p. 134
Structure the conversation and spend less time in confusing and boring meetings.

Boost team members' engagement
p. 136
Let every member be a driving force.

Increase meeting impact
p. 138
Less blah blah, more action.

Make informed decisions
p. 140
Reveal collaboration blind spots and issues with a neutral voice.

Focus the Team

Structure the conversation and spend less time in confusing and boring meetings.

The TAM can be used to close meetings and focus the team on concrete next steps. This encourages the organization of more effective meetings. Meetings have become unpopular and are considered a waste of time. But meetings are not the problem: face-to-face interaction is the best collaboration technology in the world (Dive Deeper, Impact of Communication Channels on Common Ground Creation, p. 264). The problem is what is discussed during meetings. The TAM can help by structuring the conversation in a logical order, making it easier for everyone to understand, participate, and agree on what's next.

Use the Team Alignment Map to

- Speed up interactions and save time
- Focus the discussion, reduce confusion

Timebox meetings with the TAM

1. Timebox your meeting (30, 60, 90 minutes)
2. Share the agenda
3. Discuss the topics
4. Conclude the meeting by performing a forward and a backward pass with the TAM to clarify who will do what
5. Share a photo of the TAM

The TAM can also be filled in progressively from the very beginning of the meeting. Topics are discussed and whenever a concrete action needs to be taken, a joint objective is created and a rapid forward and backward pass are performed.

Team Alignment Map

Mission: *Period:*

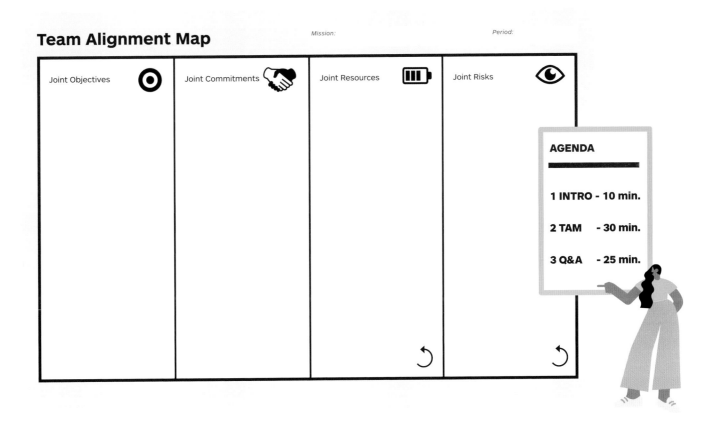

| Joint Objectives | Joint Commitments | Joint Resources | Joint Risks |

AGENDA

1 INTRO - 10 min.

2 TAM - 30 min.

3 Q&A - 25 min.

Boost Team Members' Engagement

Tired of being the team's driving force?

Frame the mission as a compelling challenge for the whole team. Lack of engagement and ownership start with a lack of participation. Frame the mission as a challenging question and let every team member respond directly on the TAM. Responding together creates a higher level of participant engagement and energy. Allowing every participant to prepare and respond in 2, 3, or 5 minutes gives everyone (in particular, introverts) a voice and fosters creativity and the perception of fairness within the team.

Use the Team Alignment Map to

• Engage team members emotionally, create a we're-all-in-this-together mindset

• Bring the team together as a real team, align personal and collective goals

Frame the mission as a challenging question

1. Frame the mission as a question, a challenge, or a problem everyone understands. Start by "How will we...,?" "How can we...?," "How to...?"
2. Ensure that everyone understands the question.
3. Allow 5 minutes for individual preparation (forward pass).
4. Allocate 2 minutes per participant to present his or her forward pass.
5. Consolidate and perform the backward pass together.

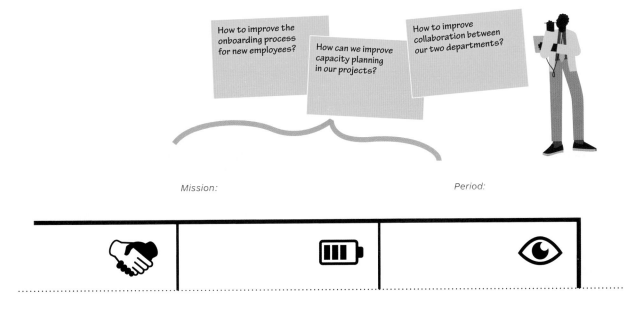

How to improve the onboarding process for new employees?

How can we improve capacity planning in our projects?

How to improve collaboration between our two departments?

Mission: *Period:*

Increase Meeting Impact

Less blah blah, more action.

No one is in charge? The objective becomes a risk. Stop blah-blah and gossip by urging the team to agree on what needs to be done and by whom. Ensure that everyone's contribution is visible on the TAM and understood and agreed on by the other team members for maximum impact. Make everyone aware of the risk that the joint objectives nobody takes care of will result in... nothing.

Use the Team Alignment Map to

- Switch from talk to action, know who does what

- Stay grounded; objectives with no commitment are considered to be risks

Switch from talk to action with clear commitments

1. Perform a forward and backward pass.
2. Ensure that every joint objective has a joint commitment; add a deadline if necessary.
3. Move all the floating objectives (with no joint commitment) into joint risks (fourth column).
4. Share a photo of the TAM.

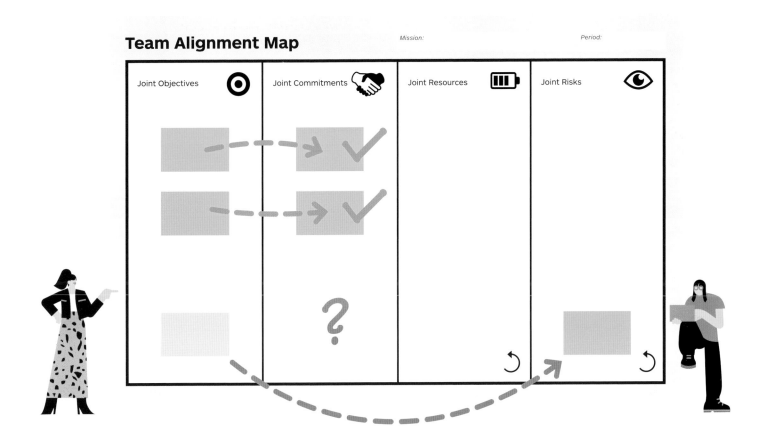

Make Informed Decisions

Reveal collaboration blind spots and issues and make better go/no go decisions.

A vote with the TAM in assessment mode can help team members to literally see their probability of success. Assessments reveal perception gaps and an aligned team will always be more likely to succeed than a misaligned team. Save your budget: assessments are fast, so don't miss an inexpensive opportunity to visualize alignment and decide whether to engage resources or if more preparation is required.

Use the Team Alignment Map to

- Proactively detect issues and reveal blind spots

- Make informed go/no go decisions, save budget

Assess team readiness and troubleshoot with the TAM

1. Run a TAM assessment (p. 104).
2. Use the vote to make a decision.

Tips

- Schedule another meeting quickly if time is short and problems can be solved reasonably fast. At the end of the second meeting, perform another assessment to confirm that issues have been addressed properly.

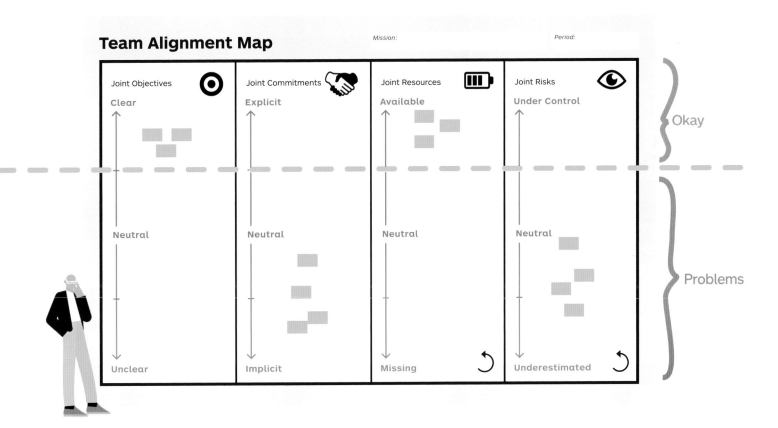

Team Alignment Map

Mission: Period:

| Joint Objectives | Joint Commitments | Joint Resources | Joint Risks |

Clear / Explicit / Available / Under Control

Neutral / Neutral / Neutral / Neutral

Unclear / Implicit / Missing / Underestimated

Okay

Problems

Case study
Humanitarian organization
36,000 employees

Do We Really Agree?

Yasmine works in a humanitarian organization headquartered in Europe. She's in charge of standardizing the HR processes worldwide with a new HR Information System (HRIS). The mission has been assigned directly by the CEO and the project involves 13 participants from five different countries. Everyone seems to agree with the CEO, but Yasmine has doubts. She decides to assess the project team with a Team Alignment Map. Was her intuition right?

Standardize salary, vacation, and contracts management in HRIS

Mission imposed by the CEO

1
Reveal

The vote reveals that the participants seem positively aligned on joint objectives, joint resources, and joint risks, but joint commitments seem to be problematic.

S. Mastrogiacomo, Missonier, and R. Bonazzi, "Talk Before It's Too Late: Reconsidering the Role of Conversation in Information Systems Project Management." Journal of Management Information Systems 31, no. 1 (2014): 47–78.

2
Reflect

Perception gaps are discussed for the joint commitments column. The team rapidly notices that commitments are not the issue. The mission is ambiguous and everyone understands it differently, so the joint objectives are too high-level. Everyone had been committing to a different interpretation of the mission, which made the problem become visible.

3
Repair

The team decides to split the current mission into three submissions and projects by creating three new Team Alignment Maps. They perform a forward and a backward pass for each and organize three validation votes after that. The votes confirm that the team is aligned and confident about what will happen next. Françoise is clearly relieved.

Pro Tips

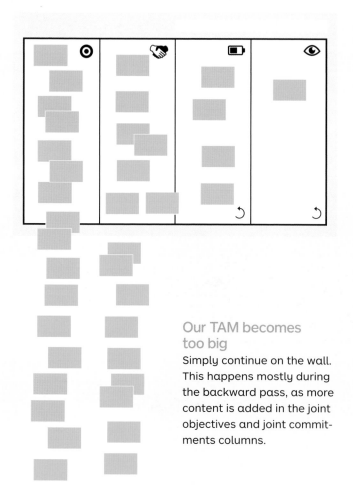

Dealing with disagreement and lack of clarity

Move unclear items to the joint risks column. The purpose of an alignment session is to create mutual clarity and agreement before people leave the meeting. When content on the TAM is perceived as ambiguous or there is disagreement in the meeting, place the item in the joint risks column for further discussion. Move it to the right column only when the content is perceived as clear and agreed on by the team.

Our TAM becomes too big

Simply continue on the wall. This happens mostly during the backward pass, as more content is added in the joint objectives and joint commitments columns.

How to manage missing stakeholders and latecomers

Take a few minutes to update briefly all latecomers so they can jump into the discussion and contribute. Team success springs from the team's common ground. Organize one-on-one update meetings when key stakeholders are missing meetings; keeping them in the loop is crucial for the team's success.

Risk identification: consider emotions as KPIs

Use fears, objections, and any emotional reactions as triggers to identify problems. We're biologically programmed to anticipate problems: fear, anger, sadness, and disgust can signal possible hidden risks. The Fact Finder (see p. 204) can help ask good questions and reveal the problems hidden behind negative emotions.

2.2
The Team Alignment Map
for Projects

Lower project risk and reduce execution problems.

Do you think we can still make it?

Techniques to Lower Project Risk and Reduce Execution Problems

Significant energy and resources are lost in projects when key stakeholders are insufficiently aligned. Information flows poorly and execution problems spiral into cost and time overruns, poor quality, or lack of client satisfaction. Creating a shared initial view of what needs to be done and maintaining a high level of alignment over time should be a priority for any project leader or manager, just as it is the duty of any stakeholder to stay informed and share new information.

√

Recommended for projects

For any project team, new or experienced. These techniques can be used independently or to complement your preferred project management tools whether you're following waterfall or agile project management principles.

×

Not recommended for operations

Not of real use for operational teams, i.e. for teams running stable, high-volume, recurring activities, unless a project is in sight.

Get Projects Off to a Good Start

It costs less than having a bad start.

The TAM can help create an initial big picture rapidly where each participant must find his or her place, whether your team is engaging in a project plan (waterfall) or a release plan (agile).

Building strong initial alignment requires additional effort, but the benefits will be tangible throughout the entire project.

Neglecting initial alignment is never a good idea. The need for coordination and crisis committees rapidly explodes in those teams that jump immediately into work with misaligned members. Nothing beats a good start when engaging in a project.

Use the Team Alignment Map to

- Give alignment an initial boost and increase the chances of success

- Gain more peace and control over the execution phases

Start projects with a TAM session

1. Create or validate alignment on who's doing what with the TAM before moving to action.
2. When initiating projects, run a TAM session. Experience tells us that it's wiser to postpone the kickoff until enough alignment is reached.

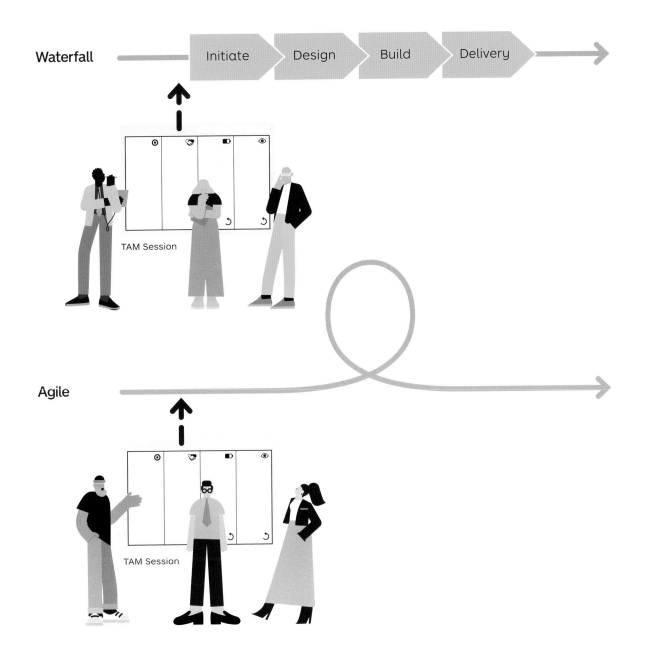

Waterfall

Initiate | Design | Build | Delivery

TAM Session

Agile

TAM Session

Maintain Alignment over Time

Staying in sync throughout the project lifecycle

Are alignment efforts similar throughout the entire project? No: in teams that have good initial alignment, the alignment efforts decrease over time — unlike teams that start projects with misaligned members and experience growing problems due to perception gaps.

Use the Team Alignment Map to

- Invest the right alignment effort at the right moment
- Avoid overcollaboration

Start projects with a TAM session

1. **Waterfall projects**: use the TAM weekly or monthly during the initiation and planning phase, and then only if required in the execution and delivery phases.
2. **Agile projects**: use a rapid TAM session at the beginning of each sprint. Sessions will become shorter over time.

Needs for alignment in Waterfall projects

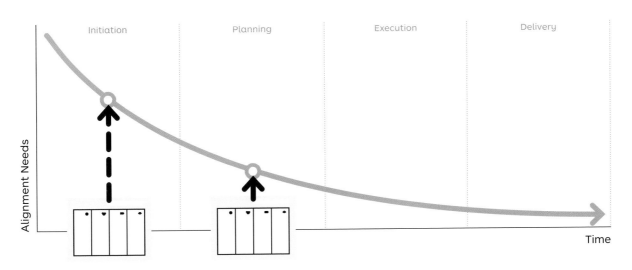

Needs for alignment in Agile projects

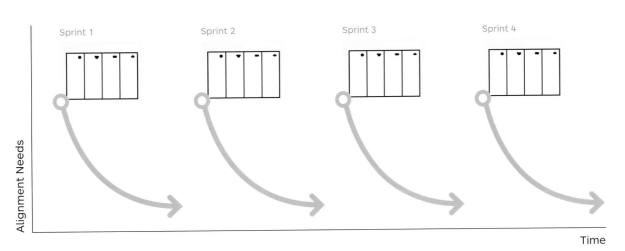

141

Four Easy Ways to Maintain Alignment with the TAM

Meeting 1
Plan

Meeting 2
Plan

Meeting N
Plan

Meeting 1
Plan

Meeting 2
Assess (Check)

Meeting N
Assess (Check)

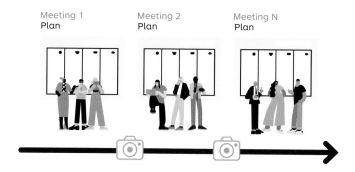

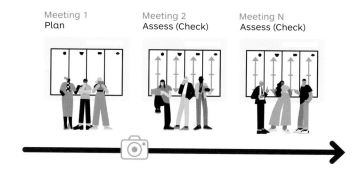

Weekly

Create an initial TAM and share a picture with all the team members. At the next session, create a new TAM for the next period by referring to the picture of the previous TAM.

Initially and with checks

Hold just one TAM session at the beginning and share a picture with the team. Perform only rapid assessments to confirm that things are on track at the end of subsequent meetings. Update the initial TAM if necessary.

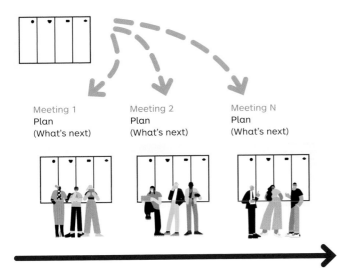

Plan
(Entire Project)

Meeting 1
Plan
(What's next)

Meeting 2
Plan
(What's next)

Meeting N
Plan
(What's next)

Meeting 1
Assess

Meeting 2
Assess

Meeting N
Assess

Entire project and weekly

A TAM is created that covers the entire project. New TAMs are created every week that cover only one week of work.

Rapid checks

For teams working with other project management tools and methods, rapid checks can be performed with the TAM at the end of key meetings.

Monitor Tasks' Progress

How to use the TAM Kanban-style to align and track work on a single wall.

Team alignment and task tracking are two different activities, and tasks are usually tracked using project management platforms. There is a low-cost solution that works for small and medium-sized projects: put a TAM on the wall and add three simple columns to simulate a Kanban board.

→

Use the Team Alignment Map to

- Align and monitor progress on a single wall

- Benefit from an easy and low-cost solution

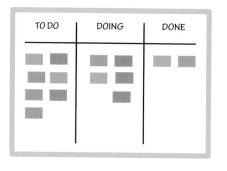

A Kanban Board offers a simple and powerful structure to monitor progress. Tasks (the colored notes) are moved between three columns: **To Do** contains the work agreed on and pending, **Doing** the tasks team members are working on, and **Done** the work that has been completed.

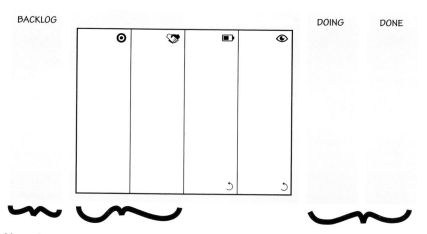

The **Backlog** column is an "inbox" to store ideas and objectives not yet discussed and validated as a team.

When combined, the joint objectives and joint commitments columns contain the **To Do** of a traditional Kanban Board.

Rest of the Kanban Board.

Monitor progress with a Team Alignment Map Kanban-style

1. Set the mission.
2. Enter new ideas and objectives in the Backlog column.
3. Perform a forward and backward pass for priority items.
4. Start moving the joint objectives combined with joint commitments (to do's) into the Doing and Done columns as team members start doing and completing their work.

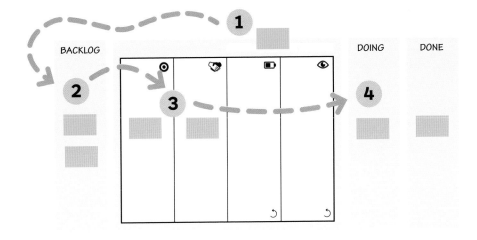

The TAM Kanban-style in Practice

Organize the wall in three main areas: Buffer, Clarify, and Track.

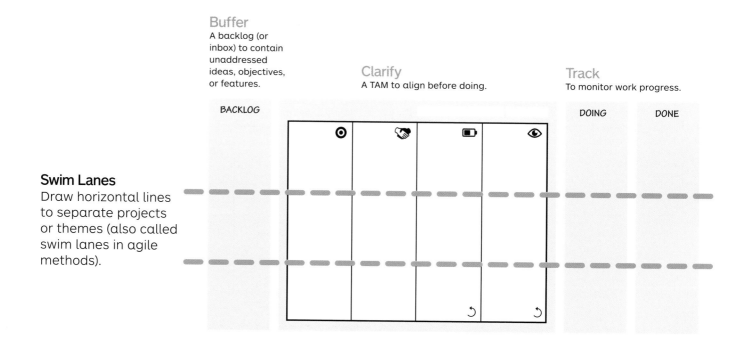

Buffer
A backlog (or inbox) to contain unaddressed ideas, objectives, or features.

Clarify
A TAM to align before doing.

Track
To monitor work progress.

BACKLOG

DOING

DONE

Swim Lanes
Draw horizontal lines to separate projects or themes (also called swim lanes in agile methods).

Example

1. The team's mission is to grow online market share. One of the pending ideas is to redesign the online store.

2. Pedro commits to improving the online store if a budget of $30K is allocated to buy the necessary licenses (forward pass).

3. Carmen, the Head of Marketing, commits to finding the budget rapidly (backward pass).

4. Carmen announces that the budget is okay and Pedro starts working on the redesign. They move their joint commitments (to do's) into the Doing and Done columns.

5. The Doing and Done columns show at any moment who's working on what and what has been completed.

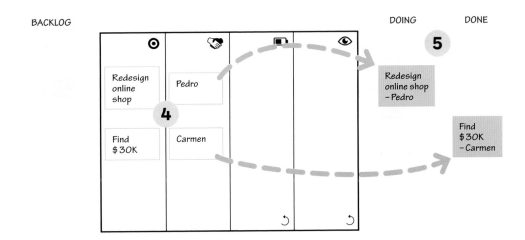

Reduce Risks (While Having Fun)

Mitigate risks visually as a team.

Project teams can neglect risk management. It's true that spending long hours filling in a projected spreadsheet line by line can be perceived as an unpleasant activity.

That exercise can become more enjoyable if done together visually during an alignment session; it's the raison d'être of the backward pass. Removing Post-it notes is removing problems — it demonstrates a tangible progression and motivates the team.

Use the Team Alignment Map to

- Mitigate project risks seamlessly
- Increase the team's accountability for risk management

Perform and emphasize the backward pass

1. Perform a forward and a backward pass for the project.
2. Insist on the backward pass: ensure that the last two columns are properly emptied and do not contain critical elements.
3. Schedule an additional meeting if you run out of time.
4. Validate as a team with a vote; share a photo of the TAM and the vote.

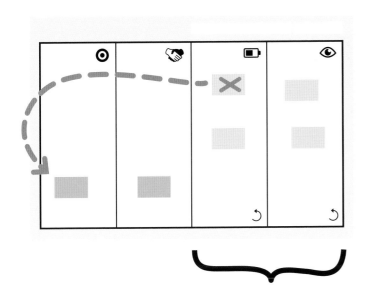

Challenge the team to empty these two columns completely.

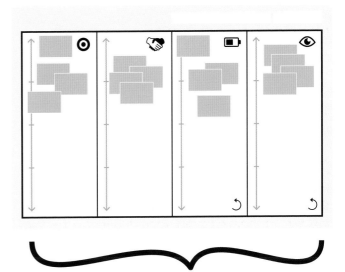

Conclude with a validation vote (the best possible validation vote is shown here).

Align Distributed Teams

Overcome the distance barrier using online boards.

Distributed teams can align remotely using online boards like Miro or Mural and benefit from great features such as:

- An infinite canvas, removing all physical constraints

- Synchronous and asynchronous collaboration

- Chat and video conferencing

- The ability to append videos and documents, add comments

On-site teams can also benefit from these features in addition to summaries of updates, version history, archiving, and integration with powerful project management tools.

Use the Team Alignment Map to

- Create a template in your preferred online board
- Create and maintain alignment remotely

Use an image of the TAM as background

1. Create a template of a TAM in your preferred online board.
2. Create and maintain alignment remotely.

Tips

- Use video conferencing in the first alignment session; it conveys nonverbal information

- Create a Team Alignment Map Kanban-style to align and monitor progress on a single board (p. 158).

- Online surveys, rather than online boards, are preferable for running TAM assessments.

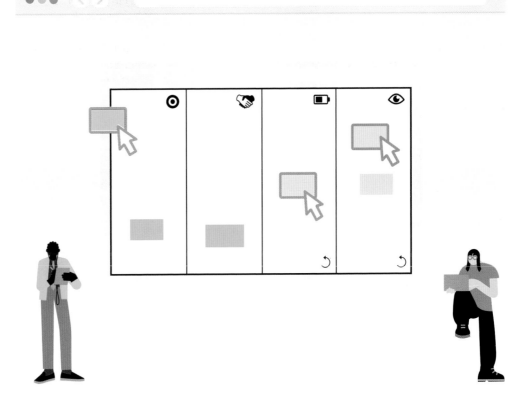

Pro Tips

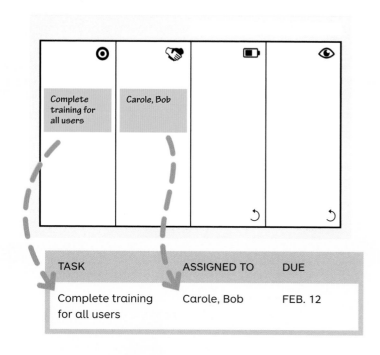

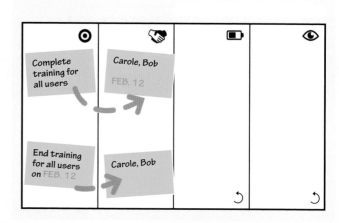

Tracking tasks with online tools

Translate objective-commitment pairs into tasks and assignments. Joint resources and joint risks can also be transferred and assigned using the same approach.

Adding delivery dates and milestones

Dates and durations can be added directly on the joint objectives or joint commitments notes. Add any milestones as joint objectives, in the first column.

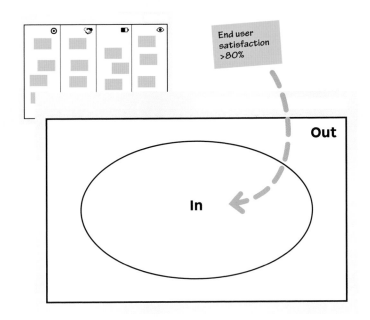

Out

In

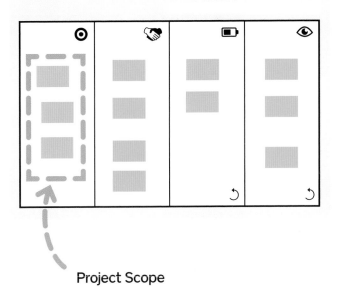

Project Scope

Adding success criteria

Use the Team Contract to discuss and hold success criteria (see p. 184). The TAM focuses on aligning on joint activities, while the Team Contract is dedicated to the rules of the game.

What if some objectives are not on the Team Alignment Map?

They are simply out of scope for that mission.

2.3

The Team Alignment Map for Organizational Alignment

Get alignment between leaders, teams, and departments to break down internal silos.

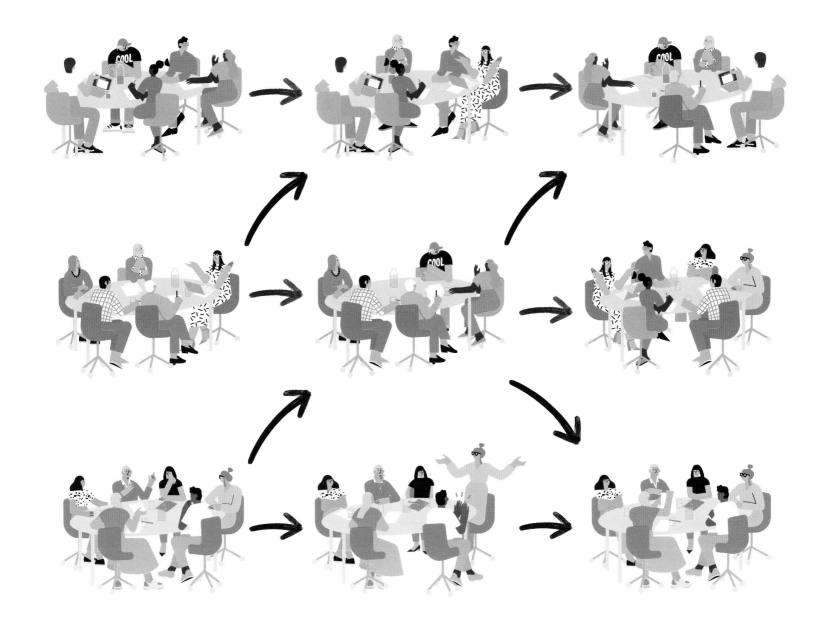

Techniques to Get Alignment Across Teams

High-caliber individuals and teams isolated in functional towers can't implement new business models, new client experiences, new products, and new services based on new processes. Complex challenges can only be addressed through effective cross-functional collaboration and participants who understand how the strategy translates into concrete, daily actions at the personal level.

Use these techniques to complement your strategy process or when launching new strategic initiatives to infuse organic alignment, facilitate cross-functional work, and engage at scale.

√

Recommended for organic change management

Create organic change by establishing a shared process and language, by empowering teams and by improving dialogue between teams and with leadership.

×

Not recommended without executive sponsorship

Make sure you are within your perimeter of legitimacy before gathering teams. The more cross-functional the initiative, the higher the level of sponsorship must be to avoid political backfires.

Empower Teams

Escape from the role of the exhausted superhero.

Teams can seriously underperform when (1) the team members can't make informed decisions because they don't understand the strategic direction and (2) the conditions/resources required for each to do their work are missing.

As a team leader, a TAM empowerment session can help you act on these two problems. You set and explain the direction (mission), the team works independently on the how (forward pass), risks are mitigated, and resources are negotiated together (backward pass).

This approach is comparable to what is coined "aligned autonomy" at Spotify, the music streaming company. Teams are empowered using this basic formula: autonomy = authority x alignment (Henrik Kniberg 2014). The mission is set by leadership (authority), the team is accountable for the how (forward and backward pass), and all this happens in a constant dialogue (alignment).

→

Use the Team Alignment Map to

- Delegate work efficiently
- Help teams self-organize, increase autonomy

Empower teams with the TAM

Roles and Responsibilities
Leaders — the what and why
- Communicate the mission: what challenge must be addressed or what problem must be solved and for what reason.
- Set short-term objectives.
- Allocate the resources required by the team.

Team(s) — the how
- Find the best solution to the problem. Optimize resource utilization.
- Collaborate with other teams if necessary.

Fast empowerment meetings with the TAM (60 minutes)

1. Mission (5 minutes): the leader assigns a clear mission to the team (what and why) and sets short-term objectives (joint objectives). The leader leaves the room and comes back for step 3.
2. Forward pass (30 minutes): the team performs a forward pass independently; accountability increases when teams self-define the "how."
3. Presentation (5 minutes): the leader is back and the team presents the forward pass.
4. Backward pass (20 minutes): performed by the team and the leader: resources are negotiated/allocated and risks are mitigated together by adding, adapting, and removing content for the TAM.
5. Validation: joint validation of the TAM by leader and team.

+

Tips

- Frame the mission as a challenge to create even more engagement (Section 2, Boost Team Members' Engagement, p. 136).
- Use the Team Contract to define "how we will collaborate" in terms of rules, process, tools, and validation points (p. 195).

Team

Leader

Engage Large Groups

How to mobilize large teams

Engagement comes from participation. Period. Mobilizing large teams requires significant energy and time, particularly if several alignment sessions are required. But it's worth every penny because the larger the group or the initiative, the greater the financial risk and the likelihood of failure. Strong initial alignment is necessary to avoid significant budget overruns and other execution disasters.

So book a large venue, divide people into subgroups, run parallel sessions to give each participant a voice, consolidate and share the results before making decisions, and move to action.

Use the Team Alignment Map to

- Increase participants' buy-in and engagement
- Reduce financial risk

Mobilizing large groups

1. Split (5 minutes): split participants in groups of 4–8.
2. Align in subteams (30 minutes): run parallel TAM sessions by assigning groups the same global mission or submissions.
3. Present (5 minutes per subteam): each group presents its TAM to all the other groups.
4. Consolidate (after the meeting): if applicable, a facilitator aggregates the results into a single TAM.
5. Share (after the meeting): consolidated results are sent to all participants, usually with a list of decisions made and for what reason.

Additional iterations are performed until enough alignment is reached. Online TAM assessments can help confirm the level alignment in large groups.

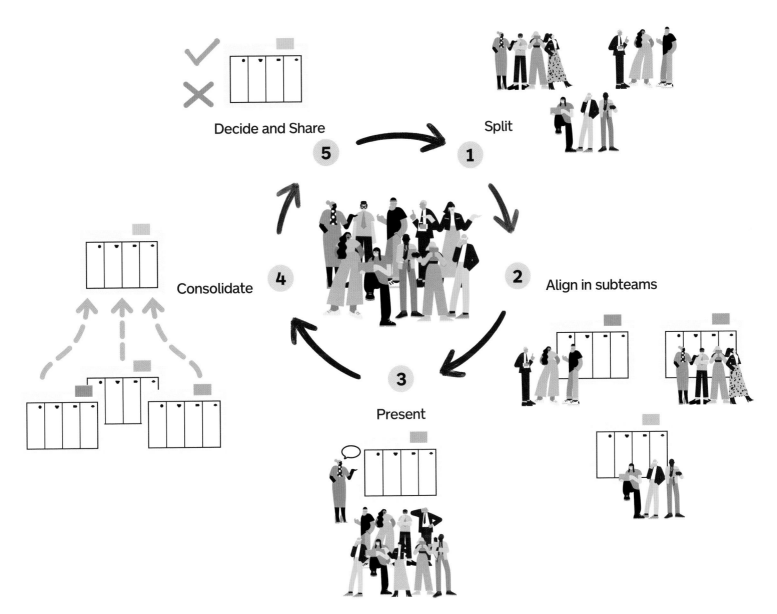

Decide and Share

Split

Consolidate

Align in subteams

Present

5

1

2

3

4

Facilitate Collaboration Across Departments and Functions

Help cross-functional teams be more successful.

When missions and objectives are misaligned within the organization, cross-functional teams get easily bogged down in unmanageable dependencies and political fights to grasp internal resources. Creating a supportive context for cross-functional work delivery starts by aligning the missions of all the impacted teams, assigning common short-term objectives, and allowing teams to discuss and negotiate shared objectives. This can be done with the TAM during alignment workshops by focusing on aligning missions and objectives with leaders and from team to team.

Use the Team Alignment Map to

- Create a shared language and process, set common goals
- Evolve the culture, implement new collaborative practices

Support Cross-Functional Work with the TAM

3 hours, up to 6 hours

1. **Mission** (10 minutes): leaders set and explain a clear global mission to the teams (what and why) and may add common joint objectives. Leaders leave the room and come back for step 3.
2. **Forward pass** (1 hour): the teams define how they will contribute to the global mission directly or by defining a submission and perform a forward pass independently.
3. **Presentations** (5 minutes per team): leaders are back and each team presents the forward pass to all the other teams, which improves the awareness of who will do what. Leaders validate the submissions, if any, and the TAMs.
4. **Backward pass and negotiation** (1 hour): resources are negotiated/allocated and risks are mitigated team to team by adding, adapting, and removing content from the TAMs. Adding new objectives can trigger a new forward and backward pass! Leaders move from group to group, clarify understanding, and take the requests.
5. **Recap and next step**: leaders recap and announce the next meeting for the feedback and decisions.

+
Tips
- Establish one or more Team Contracts to clarify or change the rules of the game (see p 184).

Aligning Missions and Goals

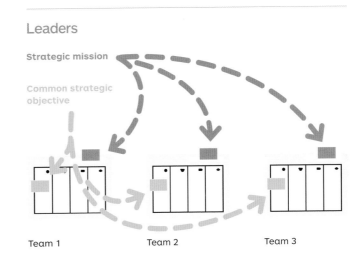

Leaders

Strategic mission

Common strategic objective

Team 1   Team 2   Team 3

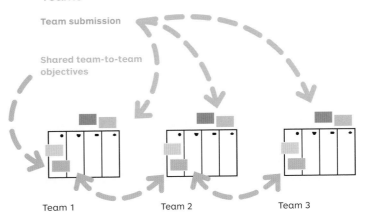

Teams

Team submission

Shared team-to-team objectives

Team 1   Team 2   Team 3

Negotiate and Allocate Resources

How to Integrate the TAM with the Business Model Canvas.

Resource negotiation is key for all projects. Whether this happens between teams or with a leader, the basic two principles remain the same:

- Gain the missing resource by explaining the relationship between the resource, the joint objectives, and the mission;

- If unsuccessful, the linked joint objective is removed or adapted.

Use the Team Alignment Map to

- Gain more resources with consistent storytelling
- Make the mission and the joint objectives more realistic

Option 1
Negotiation with leadership

- **A forward and a backward pass** are performed by the team. A presentation is scheduled with leadership to negotiate any missing resources.

- **A presentation and negotiation with leaders**: The TAM is presented in logical order to provide context. Missing resources are discussed and negotiated, and when unavailable the linked objectives are adapted or removed.

Option 2
Negotiation Team-to-Team

- **A forward and a backward pass** are performed by the teams on separate TAMs.
- **Negotiation criteria** are discussed, agreed, and prioritized between the teams before negotiating.
Criteria can be measured qualitatively (H, M, L) or quantitatively (1–5) and be equal or weighted (50%, 30%, 20%).
- **Presentation and negotiation**: teams mutually present their TAMs and tradeoffs are made team to team according to the criteria.

+

Which criteria are given the top priority?

Urgency, impact, client value, contribution to the strategy, etc. This helps avoid going around in circles and to make meaningful tradeoffs.

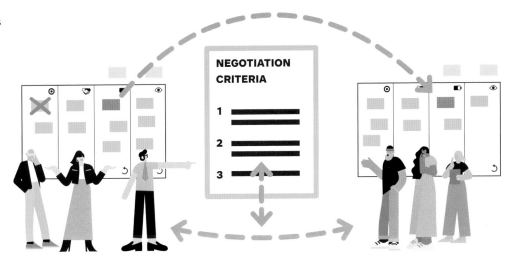

167

Integrate the TAM with Strategy Processes and Tools

Negotiate resources, peer-to-peer and with leadership.

The Team Alignment Map beautifully integrates with the Business Model Canvas (BMC) — a framework and tool to design business strategies. The strategy is operationalized by moving elements from one canvas to the other and by letting teams self-organize. This allows future contributors to feel part of the process and understand what's at stake; it also increases teams' buy-in.

Use the Team Alignment Map to

- Operationalize the strategy
- Easily integrate with the Business Model Canvas

Search keywords: business model canvas, business model generation, Alex Osterwalder

Integrate with the Business Model Canvas

1. Design the strategy with the BMC.
2. Operationalize key strategic objectives with the Team Alignment Map by:
   - Assigning missions (example: team 1)
   - Assigning objectives (example: team 2)
   - Assigning cross-cut objectives (example: teams 3 and 4)
3. Let the teams self-organize by performing a forward and a backward pass, possibly during implementation workshops where all the impacted teams are present and interact.

Additional iterations are performed until enough alignment is reached. Online TAM assessments can confirm the level alignment.

Tips

- Discuss the Key Activities of your BMC first; it's a good starting point
- Browse the rest of the canvas, looking for strategic goals to be executed

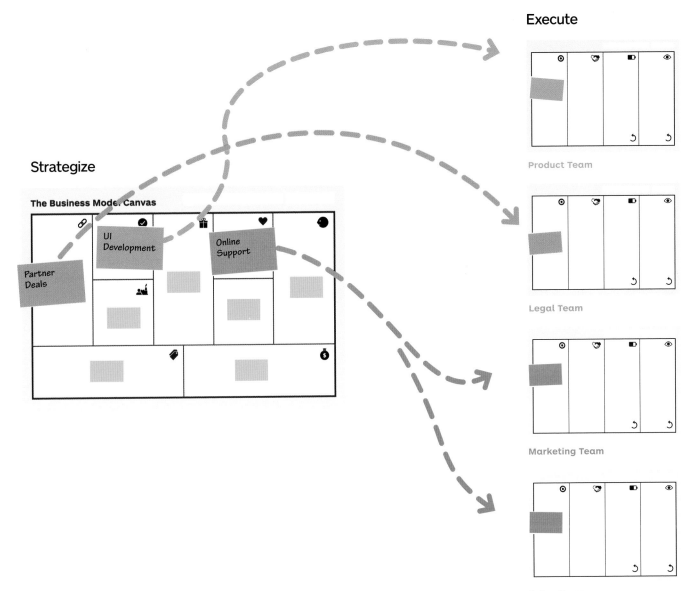

Execute

Strategize

The Business Model Canvas

Partner Deals

UI Development

Online Support

Product Team

Legal Team

Marketing Team

Sales Team

169

Assess the Readiness of Strategic Initiatives

How to assess initiatives' chances of success with hundreds of stakeholders.

Is our strategic initiative well positioned to succeed? Should we better prepare? Are any immediate decisions and actions needed?

It's not easy to capture the heartbeat of a strategic initiative with hundreds of stakeholders involved. Fast online assessments with the TAM can be run to ask hundreds of stakeholders if they think they can contribute successfully. The aggregated result gives an indication of the initiative's chances of success. It's not rocket science, but it may save your company millions. Such an assessment can be performed live with a voting platform during large coordination events, or via email using a survey tool.

Use the Team Alignment Map to

- Reduce execution risk
- Let everyone vote freely through anonymous votes

Assess online with the TAM

Run an online assessment implementing the following template in an online survey tool:

As a contributor of < *Initiative Name* >,
I find personally that the:
- Joint objectives are clear (1–5)
- Joint commitments have been defined; people and teams' roles are clear (1–5)
- Joint resources are available (1–5)
- Joint risks are under control (1–5)

1 = strongly disagree
5 = strongly agree

Online tools use horizontal sliders, so the TAM must be rotated right by 90 degrees.

Tips

- To conduct assessments by theme or group: run multiple votes, by strategic themes, by "tracks," by projects, or by teams, for a more refined assessment.

- Anonymous votes take courage: votes may reveal unexpected surprises.

Difference between paper-based and online assessments

Paper

Input

Consolidated Results

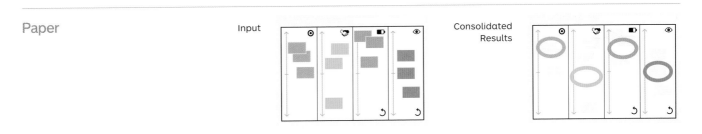

Online

Input

Consolidated Results

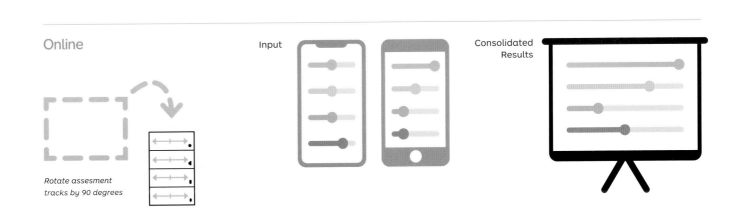

Rotate assesment tracks by 90 degrees

<u>Case study</u>
Insurance group
71,000 employees

Are We Ready to Launch Our Strategic Initiative?

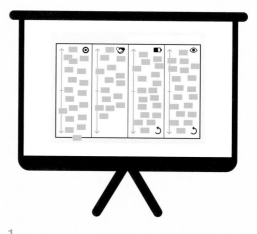

1
Reveal

The vote reveals a high level of misalignment for each variable, which is the worst-case scenario. The leadership team is surprised by the magnitude of the perception gaps.

Olivier heads an ambitious transformation program in an insurance group. The mission is to reduce costs by automating and delocalizing operational activities. The program is organized into four strategic tracks, each containing several projects. The budget is double-digits in millions. Olivier, the CEO, and the project committee fear that teams may not be ready to implement such drastic changes. Shortly before the launch of the program, they agree to assess the program readiness with 300 stakeholders.

Was the fear confirmed?

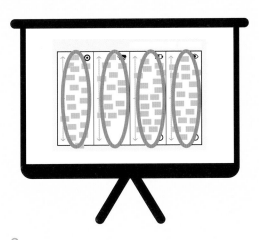

2
Reflect

The analysis discussion reveals that key parts of the program are not ready to start at all and that affects the whole vote.

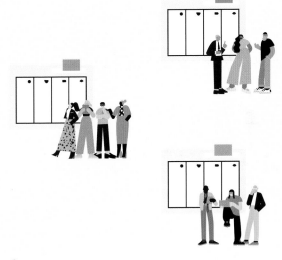

3
Repair

The launch of the whole program is postponed to an unknown date. Parallel workshops are organized to work on the problematic parts. The decision is made not to launch the program until the key problems have been solved.

The good news is that the budget is still in their hands and that significant resources haven't gone up in smoke for nothing.

Pro Tips

Successful transformation initiatives

The successful transformation programs we've experienced have these three criteria in common:

√ **Good start**: objectives are clear and key stakeholders are onboarded properly.

√ **Consistent momentum**: dates are blocked in the agendas and alignment is actively maintained.

√ **Leadership support**: there is C-level sponsorship and commitment.

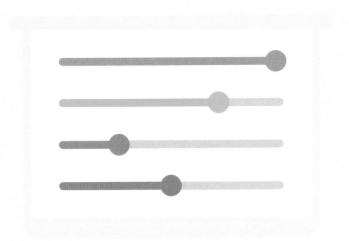

Performing assessments with large groups is easier and faster with online survey tools

Trust Among Team Members

Four tools to create a high-trust climate and increased psychological safety

"In human relations,
all prediction is
connected in one way
or another with the
phenomenon of trust."

Paul Watzlawick, Psychologist

Overview

This part introduces four add-ons to build more <u>psychological safety</u> and <u>trust</u> and create a safer team climate.

Trust and Psychological Safety Among Team Members: The Energy That Fuels the Team Alignment Map

Can a team of talents who are suspicious of each other solve complex problems together and innovate? The answer, simply, is no. Trust is a precondition for alignment.

The team doesn't engage in collective learning behaviors when people protect themselves from embarrassment and other possible threats by remaining silent. That results in poor team performance and an inability to innovate collectively. To innovate together, team members need to feel that they can talk openly and candidly to each other without fear of judgment or reprisals. Such climates are described as psychologically safe environments.

Simply put, psychological safety is a variation of trust: "The belief that the team is safe for interpersonal risk taking. That one will not be punished or humiliated for speaking up with ideas, questions, concerns, or mistakes." The term and definition were coined by Amy Edmonson, Professor of Leadership and Management at the Harvard Business School over 20 years ago in her seminal paper "Psychological Safety and Learning Behavior in Work Teams."

To learn more about Amy Edmondson's work: Dive Deeper, Trust and Psychological Safety, see p. 266

3.1
The Team Contract

Define how we work together, the principles everyone needs to know, and the behaviors that need to be respected.

3.2
The Fact Finder

Ask good questions for improving team communications, inquire like a pro to reduce perception gaps.

3.3
The Respect Card

Tips to demonstrate consideration for others.

3.4
The Nonviolent Requests Guide

Address latent conflicts and manage disagreement constructively.

3.1
The Team Contract

Define team behaviors and how we work together.

Shouldn't we have some rules in place?

Some team members
may systematically
arrive late...

...or criticize the work
of others without
suggesting alternatives.

Unspoken resentments and frustrations can accumulate and escalate into unnecessary conflict.

The Team Contract helps define the rules of the game.

The Team Contract

What are the rules and behaviors we want to abide by in our team?

The Team Contract is a simple poster used to negotiate and establish team behavior and rules, both in general or temporarily. Psychological safety is increased and potential conflict reduced by:

- Aligning relationships on appropriate and inappropriate behaviors, making the team values explicit.
- Creating a cultural base to work in harmonious conditions.
- Allowing legitimate measures in case of noncompliance.
- Preventing a sense of inequity and injustice from developing within the team.

The poster presents two trigger questions to help participants position in terms of ins — what is accepted — and outs — what should not be accepted:

1. What are the rules and behaviors we want to abide by in our team?
2. As individuals, do we have preferences for working in a certain way?

This includes topics such as team behaviors and values, decision-making rules, how to coordinate and communicate, and framing expectations in case of failure. By helping clarify expected behaviors in advance, the Team Contract offers a big payoff for a small investment of time.

The Team Contract helps:

Make values explicit — share ideas, principles, and shared beliefs as tangible behaviors.
Set the rules of the game — set clear expectations by applying a fair process.
Minimize conflict — prevent unnecessary conflict and a reference point in case of noncompliance.

→
Dive Deeper
To discover the academic backstage of the Team Contract, please read:

- Mutual Understanding and Common Ground (in Psycholinguistics), p. 264
- Relationship Types (in Evolutionary Anthropology), p. 274
- Trust and Psychological Safety (in Psychology), p. 266

The Team Contract

What are the rules and behaviors that we want to abide by in our team?
As individuals, do we have preferences for working in a certain way?

Team:

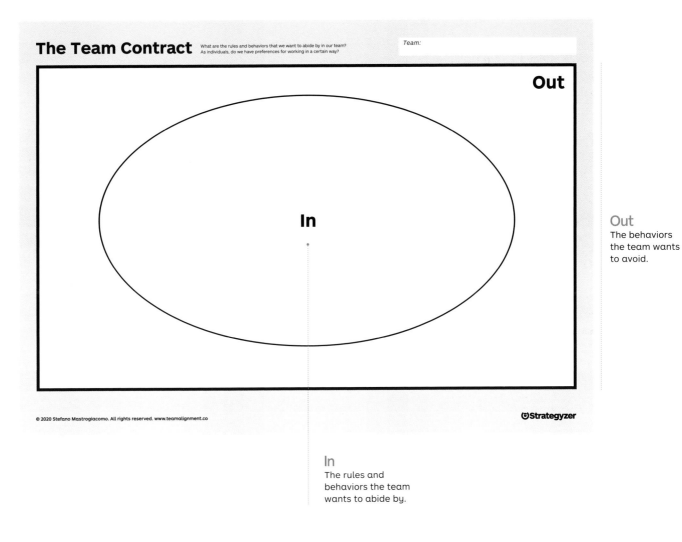

Out

In

Out
The behaviors
the team wants
to avoid.

In
The rules and
behaviors the team
wants to abide by.

Strategyzer

The Team Contract What's (Typically) In and Out?

Team Contracts are unique for each team. Expect a variety of answers as the trigger questions invite team members to position on topics covering:

- attitudes and behaviors,
- decision-making (priorities management, governance, responsibilities),
- communication (in particular, meeting management),
- the use of common tools and methods,
- disagreement and conflict management,
- relationships with other teams and departments, and so forth.

The team may also include the rewards in case of success, or the sanctions in case of noncompliance.

The Team Contract

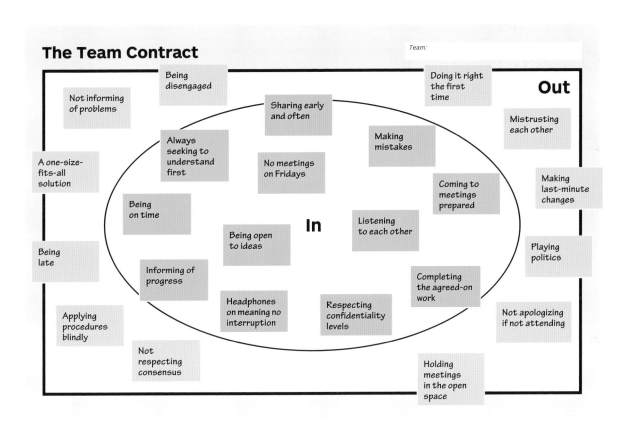

Team:

Out

In

- Being disengaged
- Not informing of problems
- Doing it right the first time
- Mistrusting each other
- Sharing early and often
- Making mistakes
- Always seeking to understand first
- No meetings on Fridays
- A one-size-fits-all solution
- Coming to meetings prepared
- Making last-minute changes
- Being on time
- Listening to each other
- Being open to ideas
- Being late
- Playing politics
- Informing of progress
- Completing the agreed-on work
- Headphones on meaning no interruption
- Respecting confidentiality levels
- Applying procedures blindly
- Not apologizing if not attending
- Not respecting consensus
- Holding meetings in the open space

Light versus Heavy Conventions

The Team Contract is a light tool to set team conventions; it binds the team morally and not legally. It can evolve later into more substantial formal and legally binding documents.

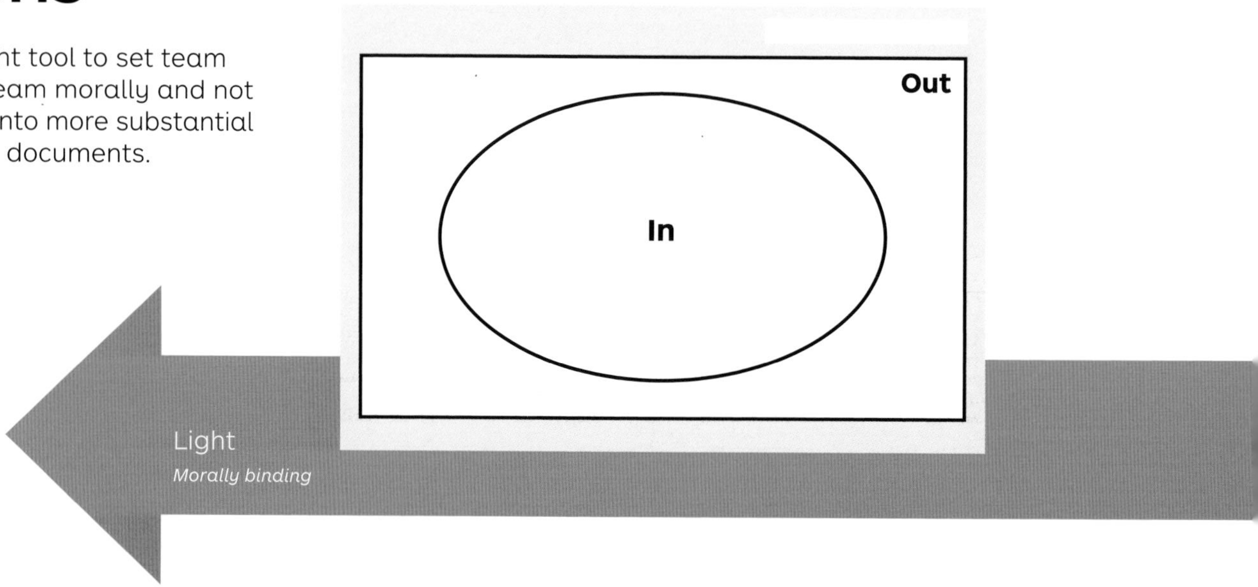

Out

In

Light
Morally binding

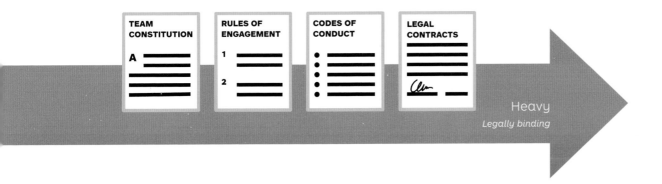

All the above documents formalize conventions between stakeholders in different contexts. *Conventions are recurring behaviors expected in recurring situations.*

How to Apply

Steps

Gather all the team members involved or all the key stakeholders in the case of a project. Place a Team Contract poster on the wall and:

1. Frame: announce the project and the period.
2. Prepare: ask every team member to respond individually to the two trigger questions in terms of possible ins and outs (5 minutes).
3. Share: allow each participant 3 minutes to present and share their answers on the poster.
4. Consolidate: open a team discussion to react, adapt, and consolidate all the content (approximately 20 minutes).
5. Validate: end the meeting when participants mutually agree on the Team Contract.

When?

As illustrated on the right, the TAM helps align everyone's contributions on a regular basis and usually requires frequent updates to reflect changes as the work is progressively delivered. The Team Contract helps establish agreements that span the entire period of the collaboration. Team Contracts are generally established at the beginning of projects, when new teams are formed, when new talents join an existing team, or when radical changes require the team to reboot its operating mode.

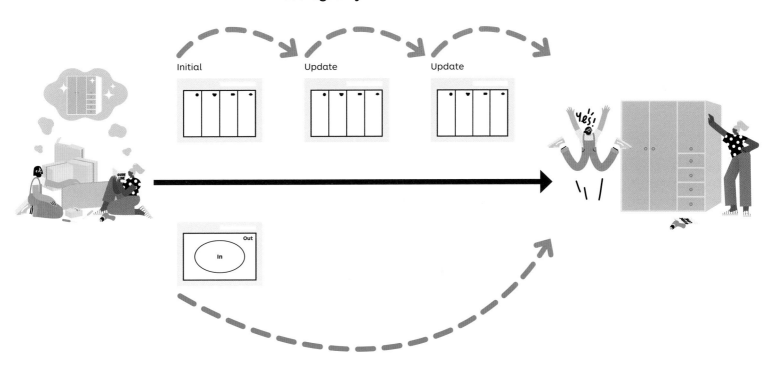

Short-term agreements
set regularly with the TAM

Initial   Update   Update

Long-term agreements
formalized with the Team Contract

A Great Team Alignment Map (TAM) Companion

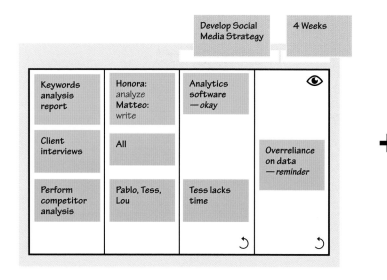

+

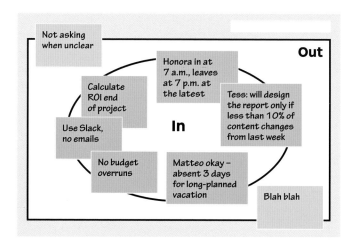

=

More alignment + more psychological safety in the team

In Case of Noncompliance

Breaches of Team Contract

Inappropriate behaviors must be confronted if a Team Contract has been violated. Avoiding confronting issues increases resentment among members who play by the rules and can affect the work and the relationships of the entire team. As a rule of thumb, this three-step approach reduces discomfort in these (sometimes difficult) conversations:

1. Explain the problem factually and refer to the Team Contract.
2. Listen carefully to all the points of view.
3. Find an appropriate solution with all the parties involved.

Resolutions are considerably facilitated when behaviors have been specified beforehand on the Team Contract. It provides a reference point, a legitimate basis for turning the problem into a learning opportunity.

Sanctioning major violations

There are behaviors that put the entire team and organization at risk, and dismissing the offender might be the most productive response. As noted by Amy Edmondson, "psychological safety is reinforced rather then harmed by fair, thoughtful responses to potentially dangerous, harmful, or sloppy behavior" (Edmondson, 2018).

Being explicit beforehand makes it easier to turn behavioral problems into learning opportunities.

When the rules are explicit and clear, everyone has a chance to play fairly. Confronting inappropriate behaviors is perceived as legitimate.

Without any explicit rules, confronting cheaters' behaviors can be perceived as unfair and trigger vengeance.

Prevent contract breaches proactively

There are pros and cons as to whether to display consequences in case of noncompliance on the Team Contract itself.

Pros: things are transparent; everyone is informed and aware of the consequences in case of non-compliance.

Cons: visible sanctions can be negatively perceived, undermine trust, and affect cooperation from the start. Consider the Prenup Paradox in psychology (Fisk and Tetlock 1997; Pinker 2008): fiancé/ées don't like to think about their upcoming marriage in terms of a possible divorce. Most couples resist prenups for good reason: the very act of discussing penalties makes it more likely that they will be needed, and that breaks the atmosphere.

Recommended: it's more diplomatic to agree on the process; for example, that noncompliance will be treated on a case-by-case basis as a team.

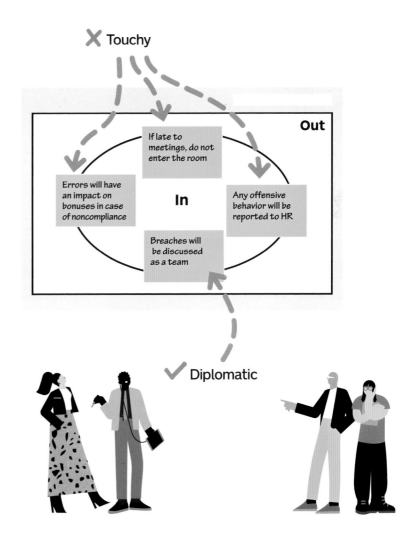

Search keywords: difficult conversations; conflict resolution techniques; HR disciplinary actions

Framing Failure Accurately on the Team Contract

Failure must be approached differently for a team working in an innovation lab and for a team working at airport security. Amy Edmondson (2018) suggests ways to frame failure accurately in three different contexts:

1. high-volume repetitive work,
2. complex operations, and
3. innovation and research.

Each context has its own different requirements in terms of error management. The table on the right shows examples for each context.

	High-volume repetitive work	Complex operations	Innovation and research
Context	• Assembly plants • Fast-food restaurants • Logistics, etc.	• Hospitals • Financial institutions • Public services, etc.	• Creating a movie • Developing new sources of energy • New product design, etc.
Constructive attitude toward failure	**Minimize preventable failures** Caused by deviations from known processes due to deficient skills, attention, or behaviors.	**Analyze and fix complex failures** Caused by unexpected events, complex systems breakdowns, etc.	**Celebrate intelligent failures** Caused by uncertainty, experimentation, and risk taking.
Examples of expectations	Train <u>all</u> new hires	Weekly risk assessment meeting	Monthly failure party and award
	Max. one defective delivery accepted per day	War room and task force setup for each system breakdown	Revise design for each failed experiment

Adapted from Amy Edmonson (2018).

3.2
The Fact Finder

Ask good questions for improving team communications.

Deploy global transformational strategies!
Incubate wireless transparency and platforms!

Sometimes, it's difficult to understand other team members and follow their logic.

The Fact Finder helps bring clarity to the conversation.

Clarify with the Fact Finder

The Fact Finder suggests questions that bring clarity to the conversation. The questions give others a chance to reformulate their thinking more accurately and to be understood.

Dive Deeper
To discover the academic back-stage of the Fact Finder, please read:

- Mutual Understanding and Common Ground (in Psycholinguistics) p. 264
- Trust and Psychological Safety (in Psychology) p. 266

The tool is built on a straightforward principle: dialogue based on concrete facts is better than dialogue based on assumptions. Engaging in such dialogue requires training as we easily tend to omit or distort information. That distortion is a direct consequence of our three-level sense-making process (Kourilsky 2014):

1. Perception: we start by perceiving a situation or we have an experience.
2. Interpretation: we give this situation an interpretation or a meaning or we form a hypothesis.
3. Evaluation: finally, what we share about the perceived situation is an evaluation, a judgment, or even a rule we inferred.

Confusing these levels leads us directly into one (or several) of the five following communication traps:

1. Unclear facts or experiences: an absence of key information in the description.
2. Generalizations: when we turn a particular case into a universal law.

3. Assumptions: creative interpretations of an experience or situation.
4. Limitations: imaginary restrictions and obligations that narrow down options.
5. Judgements: subjective assessments of a thing, a situation, or a person.

These traps illustrate the difference between what psychologists call first-order reality and second-order realities:
A first-order reality is made up of the physically observable qualities — through our five senses — of a thing or a situation.
Second-order realities are personal interpretations of a first-order reality (judgments, hypotheses, assumptions, etc.).

For example, Ann can say "I'm hungry" (factual communication, a first-order reality) or loudly claim "we always eat too late," which is a judgment (a second-order reality) to express the fact that she's hungry. The second statement causes communication problems that can lead to conflicts,

blockages, and dead ends (Kourilsky 2014) and is mostly visible when we start arguing with each other.

By helping understand the facts (first-order reality) hidden behind ambiguous second-order statements (second-order realities), the Fact Finder makes the dialogue more productive and efficient.

The Fact Finder helps:

Inquire like a pro — identify and overcome common language traps.
Better information and decisions — clarify what is said: what others are saying and also what you are saying.
Save efforts — engage in shorter and more efficient dialogue.

The Fact Finder

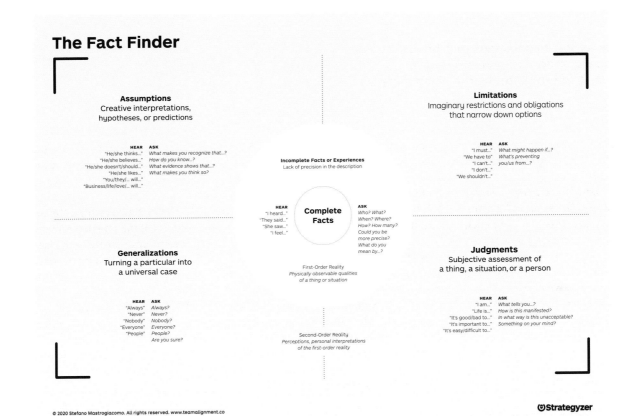

Assumptions
Creative interpretations,
hypotheses, or predictions

HEAR | ASK
"He/she thinks..." — What makes you recognize that...?
"He/she believes..." — How do you know...?
"He/she doesn't/should..." — What evidence shows that...?
"He/she likes..." — What makes you think so?
"You/they/... will..."
"Business/life/love/... will..."

Limitations
Imaginary restrictions and obligations
that narrow down options

HEAR | ASK
"I must..." — What might happen if...?
"We have to" — What's preventing
"I can't..." — you/us from...?
"I don't..."
"We shouldn't..."

Incomplete Facts or Experiences
Lack of precision in the description

HEAR
"I heard..."
"They said..."
"She saw..."
"I feel..."

Complete Facts

ASK
Who? What?
When? Where?
How? How many?
Could you be
more precise?
What do you
mean by...?

First-Order Reality
*Physically observable qualities
of a thing or situation*

Generalizations
Turning a particular into
a universal case

HEAR | ASK
"Always" — Always?
"Never" — Never?
"Nobody" — Nobody?
"Everyone" — Everyone?
"People" — People?
Are you sure?

Second-Order Reality
*Perceptions, personal interpretations
of the first-order reality*

Judgments
Subjective assessment of
a thing, a situation, or a person

HEAR | ASK
"I am..." — What tells you...?
"Life is..." — How is this manifested?
"It's good/bad to..." — In what way is this unacceptable?
"It's important to..." — Something on your mind?
"It's easy/difficult to..."

Strategyzer

The Five Communication Traps Illustrated

He can relate his experience factually.

"Yesterday I saw someone eating three burgers at the local fast-food restaurant."

1
Original Situation
Ivan sees someone eating three burgers at the local fast-food restaurant.

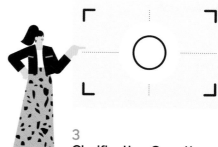

3
Clarification Questions
Clarification questions help understand the facts and the experiences (first-order reality) behind the personal interpretations (second-order realities). This moves the conversation from the ambiguity and fuzziness of the gray area to the clarity of facts, i.e. to the central white area.

2

Communication Traps

Ivan can also fall into one of these traps
when relating his experience.

Assumptions

*"Yesterday I saw someone who
had not eaten for two weeks!"*

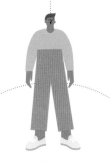

Incomplete Facts
or Experiences

*"Yesterday I saw
someone eating."*

Limitations

"Burgers must be banned."

Generalizations

"People eat a lot."

Judgments

"Eating three burgers is bad."

213

In Practice

Use of the Fact Finder occurs
in two steps:

1. Hear: identify the trap: are you hearing an
   assumption, a limitation, a generalization,
   a judgment, or incomplete facts?
2. Ask: use one of the suggested clarifying
   questions to bring the conversation back
   to the center, i.e. complete facts and
   experiences.

Clarifying question are neutral — they do
not convey any form of judgment — and
open — they don't trigger closed binary
responses (yes/no).

Clarify Incomplete Facts or Experiences
Questions help specify the facts further.

Hear
"I heard…"
"They said…"
"She saw…"
"I feel…"

Ask
Who? What?
When? Where?
How? How many?
Could you be
more precise?
What do you
mean by…?

*The designers
told me they
need more
time.*

*Could you be
more precise?*

Clarify Assumptions

Questions help disentangle
the causal links.

Hear
"He/she thinks…"
"He/she
believes…"
"He/she doesn't/
should…"
"He/she likes…"
"You/they/…
will…"
"Business/life/
love/… will…"

Ask
What makes you recognize that…?
How do you know…?
What evidence shows that…?
What makes you think so?

*I think if we
receive the
materials in
two days the
entire project
will be delayed
by two months.*

*How can two
days cause
a two-month
delay?*

Clarify Limitations

Questions help identify the
cause or the consequences
of the belief.

Hear
"I must…"
"We have to"
"I can't…"
"I don't…"
"We
shouldn't…"

Ask
What might happen if…?
What's preventing
you/us from…?

*I can't, we
never worked
like this here,
it's not in our
DNA.*

*Sure, and if
you did, what
would happen?*

Clarify Generalizations

Questions help reveal
a counterexample.

Hear
"Always"
"Never"
"Nobody"
"Everyone"
"People"

Ask
Always?
Never?
Nobody?
Everyone?
People ?
Are you sure?

*Risks are high,
everyone is so
demotivated.*

Everyone?

Clarify Judgments

Questions help reveal the
assessment criteria behind
the judgment.

Hear
"I am…"
"Life is…"
"It's good/bad
to…"
"It's important
to…"
"It's easy/
difficult to…"

Ask
What tells you…?
How is this manifested?
In what way is this
unacceptable?
Something on your mind?

*It's important
we achieve my
objectives first.*

*Well, what tells
you that?*

In Summary

Communication traps
Clarification Questions Help...

Incomplete facts or experiences
Lack of precision in the description.
Specify the facts further.

Assumptions
Creative interpretations, hypotheses, or predictions.
Disentangle the causal links.

Generalizations
Turning a particular into a universal case.
Reveal a counterexample.

Limitations
Imaginary restrictions and obligations that
narrow down options.
Identify the cause or the consequences of the belief.

Judgments
Subjective assessment of a thing, a situation, or a person.
Reveal the assessment criteria.

Origins of the Fact Finder
The Fact Finder has its roots in
neuro-linguistic programming
(NLP), a therapeutic communication approach developed by
John Grinder and Richard Bandler.
They named their framework
the "metamodel." Implementing
the metamodel turned out to
be quite challenging and led
coach Alain Cayrol to develop
a more applicable version he
called the Language Compass.
The Language Compass has
been subsequently improved and
extended by Françoise Kourilsky,
a French psychologist who inspired
the design of the Fact Finder.

*Search keywords: NLP, meta-
model, powerful questions, clear
questions*

The Fact Finder

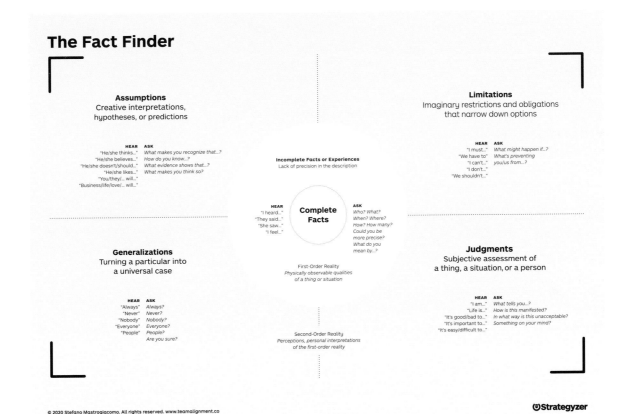

Assumptions
Creative interpretations, hypotheses, or predictions

HEAR | **ASK**
"He/she thinks..." | *What makes you recognize that...?*
"He/she believes..." | *How do you know...?*
"He/she doesn't/should..." | *What evidence shows that...?*
"He/she likes..." | *What makes you think so?*
"You/they/... will..."
"Business/life/love/... will..."

Limitations
Imaginary restrictions and obligations that narrow down options

HEAR | **ASK**
"I must..." | *What might happen if...?*
"We have to" | *What's preventing*
"I can't..." | *you/us from...?*
"I don't..."
"We shouldn't..."

Incomplete Facts or Experiences
Lack of precision in the description

HEAR | **Complete Facts** | **ASK**
"I heard..." | | *Who? What?*
"They said..." | | *When? Where?*
"She saw..." | | *How? How many?*
"I feel..." | | *Could you be more precise? What do you mean by...?*

First-Order Reality
Physically observable qualities of a thing or situation

Generalizations
Turning a particular into a universal case

HEAR | **ASK**
"Always" | *Always?*
"Never" | *Never?*
"Nobody" | *Nobody?*
"Everyone" | *Everyone?*
"People" | *People? Are you sure?*

Judgments
Subjective assessment of a thing, a situation, or a person

HEAR | **ASK**
"I am..." | *What tells you...?*
"Life is..." | *How is this manifested?*
"It's good/bad to..." | *In what way is this unacceptable?*
"It's important to..." | *Something on your mind?*
"It's easy/difficult to..."

Second-Order Reality
Perceptions, personal interpretations of the first-order reality

Ⓦ**Strategyzer**

Pro Tips

Adapt the clarification questions
Adapt the wording to the context and situation to avoid being perceived as a robot. The Fact Finder has questions that may give the conversation an unnatural twist.

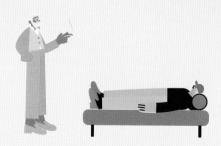

Don't
Repeat questions as they are

Do
Adapt to the context and situation

Stop justifying yourself and save energy
Stop justifying and ask a clarification question. Launching into long and visibly unconvincing justifications signals that it's time to use the Fact Finder. It will save everyone's energy and time.

Don't
Lose energy in justifications

Do
Ask a clarification question

**Avoid closed-ended questions
when inquiring**

The Fact Finder contains only open-ended
questions. Open-ended questions don't
trigger a mere yes/no, which helps others
develop their thinking.

Don't
Closed-ended questions
don't help inquire

Do
Open-ended questions
give access to the other's
thoughts

Limits of the Fact Finder

Overuse of the Fact Finder will be perceived
as intrusive and irritating. Use it mainly
when you feel lost and find it difficult to
understand the other person's logic.

Don't
Overusing the Fact Finder
can make you look intrusive

Do
Use it primarily to
clarify messages

3.3
The Respect Card

Demonstrate consideration for others by practicing
basic politeness rules.

No, no, I'm listening.

Lack of tact in interpersonal relationships makes teamwork slower and harder.

The Respect Card suggests ways to express consideration for others and maintain a respectful climate.

The Respect Card

The Respect Card gives tips for valuing others and expressing respect. Use it to prepare for meetings or when writing messages to people:
- You're not familiar with,
- With whom you feel less confident such as strangers, acquaintances, newcomers to the team, superiors, or
- With different cultural backgrounds.

The use of these hints demonstrates our ability to consider the identity and feelings of others (Brown 2015) and contributes to the creation of more psychological safety and harmony in teams.

The tool presents two checklists:
1. Tips for showing that you value and care for others (on the right)
2. Tips for demonstrating respect by minimizing requests and the likelihood of offending others (on the left)

The Respect Card is grounded in face and politeness theory; all tips present techniques to avoid causing others to lose face in public. The main focus is on language; the card presents only limited behaviors or good manners, such as not interrupting or not listening while someone is talking.

The Respect Card helps:

Get messages across with respect — challenge the status quo with respect.

Value others — by expressing consideration and gratitude.

Avoid unintentional gaffes — when dealing with strangers or power relationships.

Dive Deeper
To discover the academic backstage of the Respect Card, please read:
- Face and Politeness (in Psycholinguistics), p. 282
- Trust and Psychological Safety (in Psychology), p. 266

The Respect Card Tips for tactful communication.

Need to be respected
Demonstrate Respect

Questioning rather than commanding
Will you...?

Express doubt
I don't suppose you might...?

Hedge the request
..., if possible.

Acknowledge the impingement
I'm sure you're busy, but...

Indicate reluctance
I normally wouldn't ask, but...

Apologize
I'm sorry to bother you, but...

Acknowledge a debt
I'd be grateful if you would...

Use honorifics
Mr., Mrs., Miss, Professor, Dr. etc...

Be indirect
I'm looking for a pen.

Request forgiveness
You must forgive me but...
Could I borrow your pen?

Minimize request
I just wanted to ask you if I could use your pen.

Pluralize the person responsible
We forgot to tell you that you needed
to buy your plane ticket by yesterday.

Hesitate
Can I, uh,...?

Impersonalize
Smoking is not permitted.

RISKY BEHAVIORS
Direct orders
Interrupt
Give warnings
Prohibit
Threaten
Suggestions
Reminders
Advice

Need to be valued
Demonstrate Recognition

Thank
A big thank you.

Wish
Be well, have a nice day.

Inquire
How are you? How is it going?

Compliment
Nice sweater.

Anticipate
You must be hungry.

Advice
Take care.

Endear
My friend, mate, buddy, pal, honey, dear, bro, guys.

Solicit agreement
You know?

Attend to others
You must be hungry, it's been a long
time since breakfast. How about some lunch?

Avoid disagreement
A: You don't like it?
B: Yes, yes I like it, um, I usually don't eat this but it's good.

Assume agreement
So, when are you coming to see us?

Hedge opinion
You really should sort of try harder.

RISKY BEHAVIORS
Embarrass
Disapprove
Ignore
Openly criticize
Contempt, ridicule
Speak only about yourself
Mention taboo topics
Insults, accusations, complaints

⊘Strategyzer

Respect
Use these "social
breaks" to avoid gaffes
and express respect

Recognition
Use these "social
accelerators" to
value others.

The Respect Card
Tips for tactful communication.

Need to be respected
Demonstrate Respect

Questioning rather than commanding
Will you...?

Express doubt
I don't suppose you might...?

Hedge the request
..., if possible.

Acknowledge the impingement
I'm sure you're busy, but...

Indicate reluctance
I normally wouldn't ask, but...

Apologize
I'm sorry to bother you, but...

Acknowledge a debt
I'd be grateful if you would...

Use honorifics
Mr., Mrs., Miss, Professor, Dr. etc...

Be indirect
I'm looking for a pen.

Request forgiveness
You must forgive me but...
Could I borrow your pen?

Minimize request
I just wanted to ask you if I could use your pen.

Pluralize the person responsible
*We forgot to tell you that you needed
to buy your plane ticket by yesterday.*

Hesitate
Can I, uh,...?

Impersonalize
Smoking is not permitted.

RISKY BEHAVIORS
Direct orders
Interrupt
Give warnings
Prohibit
Threaten
Suggestions
Reminders
Advice

How to Express Respect

✓

Face is saved

The indirect request helps minimize the imposition to remove the objectives.

✕

Face is not saved

The direct request is perceived as an order; the team might feel offended.

How to Value Others

√
Face is saved

The request is delivered by
demonstrating appreciation.

×
Face is not saved

The requests are presented as
a criticism or a judgment.

Need to be valued
Demonstrate Recognition

Thank
A big thank you.

Wish
Be well, have a nice day.

Inquire
How are you? How is it going?

Compliment
Nice sweater.

Anticipate
You must be hungry.

Advice
Take care.

Endear
My friend, mate, buddy, pal, honey, dear, bro, guys.

Solicit agreement
You know?

Attend to others
You must be hungry, it's been a long time since breakfast. How about some lunch?

Avoid disagreement
A: You don't like it?
B: Yes, yes I like it, um, I usually don't eat this but it's good.

Assume agreement
So, when are you coming to see us?

Hedge opinion
You really should sort of try harder.

RISKY BEHAVIORS
Embarrass
Disapprove
Ignore
Openly criticize
Contempt, ridicule
Speak only about yourself
Mention taboo topics
Insults, accusations, complaints

How to

Use the Respect Card to prepare
for an oral or written communication

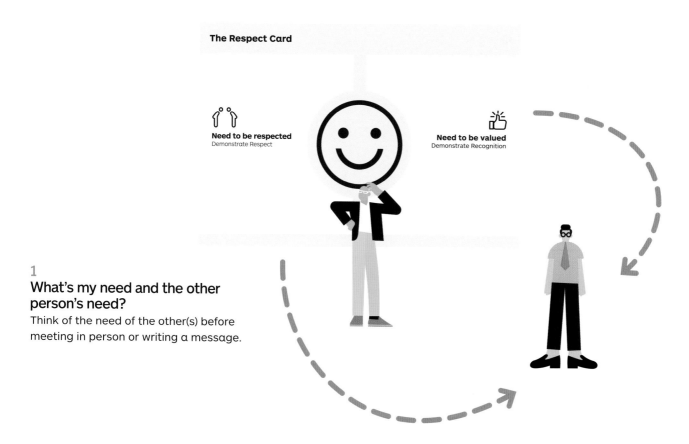

The Respect Card

Need to be respected
Demonstrate Respect

Need to be valued
Demonstrate Recognition

1
What's my need and the other person's need?
Think of the need of the other(s) before meeting in person or writing a message.

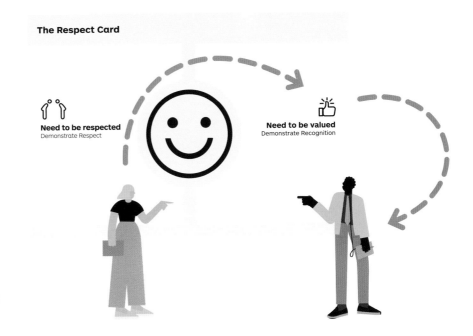

The Respect Card

Need to be respected
Demonstrate Respect

Need to be valued
Demonstrate Recognition

2

Find ideas in the two checklists for ideas before speaking or writing

Browse the techniques to gain ideas;
pick and use the most appropriate.

Pro Tips

Politeness depends on the situation, context, and culture
Consideration requires discernment. For example, a simple "thank you" can be perceived as either politeness or sarcasm.

Politeness
Thank you.

Sarcasm
Thank you.

Meet privately for sensitive topics
Private meetings are preferable when you or the other is in the hot seat; everyone will only be better off. Public embarrassment or humiliation push the resentment button and trigger revenge.

Private
I'm surprised!

Public
I'm surprised!

The Respect Card is not for every situation
Urgent situations require direct instructions; polite language is ambiguous and inefficient for coordinating when things are urgent.

Direct request
Bring the extinguisher!

Indirect request
I was wondering if you might possibly pass me the fire extinguisher?

Impoliteness: extremes meet extremes
Being rude or overpolite are both perceived as negative and inappropriate behaviors (Locher and Watts 2008).

Rude
That's bad work.

Overly polite
Your highness, I would be eternally grateful if you could envision the possibility to forgive me for daring asking you an incredibly little favor.

3.4
The Nonviolent Requests Guide

Address latent conflicts and manage disagreement constructively.

Poor management of disagreements can damage relationships and result in unrecoverable costs.

The Nonviolent Requests Guide helps
manage conflict constructively.

The Nonviolent Requests Guide

The Nonviolent Requests Guide helps prepare and express discontent constructively. The guide presents a simplified version of the nonviolent communication (NVC) principles developed by psychologist Marshall Rosenberg. As he writes: "When we express our needs indirectly through the use of evaluations, interpretations, and images, others are likely to hear criticism. And when people hear anything that sounds like criticism, they tend to invest their energy in self-defense or counterattack" (Rosenberg 2003).

By suggesting a structure for making non-judgmental requests, disagreement can be expressed without making others feel personally attacked; this creates an opportunity for empathic dialogue and conflict resolution.

Nonviolent communication (NVC) is a powerful framework and one of the key tools behind Microsoft's cultural transformation and product renewal. When Satya Nadella became the company CEO, one of his first acts was to ask top executives to read Rosenberg's book (McCracken 2017).

The Nonviolent Requests Guide helps:

Express disagreement constructively — share your view without blaming or criticizing.

Resolve conflicts — create a win-win context.

Strengthen relationships — contribute to a safer team climate.

→

To discover the academic backstage of the Nonviolent Requests Guide, please read:

- Nonviolent Communication (in Psychology), p. 249
- Trust and Psychological Safety (in Psychology), p. 266

The Nonviolent Requests Guide

Feelings *negative feelings when your needs are not satisfied*

AFRAID	CONFUSED	EMBARRASSED	SAD
apprehensive	ambivalent	ashamed	depressed
dread	baffled	chagrined	dejected
foreboding	bewildered	flustered	despair
frightened	dazed	guilty	despondent
mistrustful	hesitant	mortified	disappointed
panicked	lost	self-conscious	discouraged
petrified	mystified		disheartened
scared	perplexed	**TENSE**	forlorn
suspicious	puzzled	anxious	gloomy
terrified	torn	cranky	heavy hearted
wary		distressed	hopeless
worried	**DISCONNECTED**	distraught	melancholy
	alienated	edgy	unhappy
ANNOYED	aloof	fidgety	wretched
aggravated	apathetic	frazzled	
dismayed	bored	irritable	**VULNERABLE**
disgruntled	cold	jittery	fragile
displeased	detached	nervous	guarded
exasperated	indifferent	overwhelmed	helpless
frustrated	numb	restless	insecure
impatient	removed	stressed out	leery
irritated	uninterested		reserved
irked	withdrawn	**PAIN**	sensitive
		agony	
ANGRY	**DISQUIET**	anguished	**YEARNING**
enraged	agitated	bereaved	envious
furious	alarmed	devastated	jealous
incensed	disconcerted	grief	longing
indignant	disturbed	heartbroken	nostalgic
irate	perturbed	hurt	pining
livid	rattled	lonely	wistful
outraged	restless	miserable	
resentful	shocked	regretful	
	startled	remorseful	
AVERSION	surprised		
animosity	troubled	**FATIGUE**	
appalled	turbulent	beat	
contempt	turmoil	burnt out	
disgusted	uncomfortable	depleted	
dislike	uneasy	exhausted	
hate	unnerved	lethargic	
horrified	unsettled	listless	
hostile	upset	sleepy	
repulsed		tired	
		weary	
		worn out	

When you do

_____
OBSERVATION

I feel

_____
FEELING

My need is

_____
NEED

Would you please

_____ ?
REQUEST

Needs

CONNECTION	PHYSICAL WELL-BEING	AUTONOMY
acceptance	air	choice
affection	food	freedom
appreciation	movement/	independence
belonging	exercise	space
cooperation	rest/sleep	spontaneity
communication	safety	
closeness	shelter	**MEANING**
community	touch	awareness
companionship	water	celebration of life
compassion		challenge
consideration	**HONESTY**	clarity
consistency	authenticity	competence
empathy	integrity	consciousness
inclusion	presence	contribution
intimacy		creativity
love	**PLAY**	discovery
mutuality	joy	efficacy
nurturing	humor	effectiveness
respect/self-respect		growth
safety	**PEACE**	hope
security	beauty	learning
stability	communication	mourning
support	ease	participation
to know and be known	equality	purpose
to see and be seen	harmony	self-expression
to understand	inspiration	stimulation
trust	order	to matter
warmth		understanding

Formulation Aids
A list of unsatisfied feelings and needs for a more accurate description.

The Request
A template to prepare the nonviolent request.

⊕Strategyzer

In Practice

A nonviolent statement is composed of four consecutive parts (Rosenberg 2003):

The guide proposes a template to formulate the request and a list designed by the Center for Nonviolent Communication to convey feelings and needs more accurately.

How to formulate a nonviolent request?
1. **When you do [observation],**
2. **I feel [feeling].**
3. **My need is [need],**
4. **Would you please [request]?**

Example
"Do you ever say thank you?"

Nonviolent statement:
1. When you do [*compliment everyone in the team but me*],
2. I feel [*disappointed*].
3. My need is [*that my work is appreciated*],
4. Would you please [*help me understand if something is wrong with me*]?

Adapted from Rosenberg (2003).

The Nonviolent Requests Guide

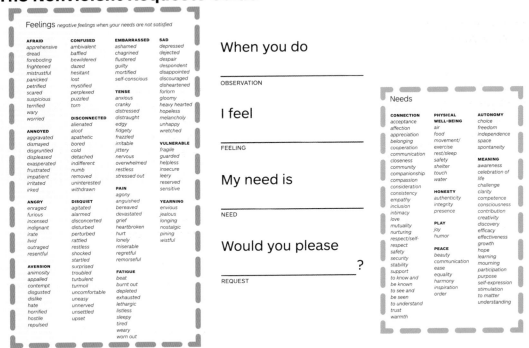

Feelings *negative feelings when your needs are not satisfied*

AFRAID
apprehensive
dread
foreboding
frightened
mistrustful
panicked
petrified
scared
suspicious
terrified
wary
worried

ANNOYED
aggravated
dismayed
disgruntled
displeased
exasperated
frustrated
impatient
irritated
irked

ANGRY
enraged
furious
incensed
indignant
irate
livid
outraged
resentful

AVERSION
animosity
appalled
contempt
disgusted
dislike
hate
horrified
hostile
repulsed

CONFUSED
ambivalent
baffled
bewildered
dazed
hesitant
lost
mystified
perplexed
puzzled
torn

DISCONNECTED
alienated
aloof
apathetic
bored
cold
detached
indifferent
numb
removed
uninterested
withdrawn

DISQUIET
agitated
alarmed
disconcerted
disturbed
perturbed
rattled
restless
shocked
startled
surprised
troubled
turbulent
turmoil
uncomfortable
uneasy
unnerved
unsettled
upset

EMBARRASSED
ashamed
chagrined
flustered
guilty
mortified
self-conscious

TENSE
anxious
cranky
distressed
distraught
edgy
fidgety
frazzled
irritable
jittery
nervous
overwhelmed
restless
stressed out

PAIN
agony
anguished
bereaved
devastated
grief
heartbroken
hurt
lonely
miserable
regretful
remorseful

FATIGUE
beat
burnt out
depleted
exhausted
lethargic
listless
sleepy
tired
weary
worn out

SAD
depressed
dejected
despair
despondent
disappointed
discouraged
disheartened
forlorn
gloomy
heavy hearted
hopeless
melancholy
unhappy
wretched

VULNERABLE
fragile
guarded
helpless
insecure
leery
reserved
sensitive

YEARNING
envious
jealous
longing
nostalgic
pining
wistful

When you do

_____
OBSERVATION

I feel

_____
FEELING

My need is

_____
NEED

Would you please

_____?
REQUEST

Needs

CONNECTION
acceptance
affection
appreciation
belonging
cooperation
communication
closeness
community
companionship
compassion
consideration
consistency
empathy
inclusion
intimacy
love
mutuality
nurturing
respect/self-respect
safety
security
stability
support
to know and be known
to see and be seen
to understand
trust
warmth

PHYSICAL WELL-BEING
air
food
movement/exercise
rest/sleep
safety
shelter
touch
water

HONESTY
authenticity
integrity
presence

PLAY
joy
humor

PEACE
beauty
communication
ease
equality
harmony
inspiration
order

AUTONOMY
choice
freedom
independence
space
spontaneity

MEANING
awareness
celebration of life
challenge
clarity
competence
consciousness
contribution
creativity
discovery
efficacy
effectiveness
growth
hope
learning
mourning
participation
purpose
self-expression
stimulation
to matter
understanding

⊕ Strategyzer

Attacks versus Nonviolent Requests

Attacks

You're always late!
I can't count on you!

Am I the only person
working here?

Are we done?
I have work to do.

Situation

Overdue work	Work Overload	Meeting Attendance
• When you do [*tell me at the last minute that your work is not ready*], • I feel [*furious*]. • My need is [*to respect the deadlines we've committed to*], • Would you please [*inform me in advance in case of a problem*]?	• When you do [*hold me accountable for all these objectives*], • I feel [*overwhelmed because good design takes time*]. • My need is [*to ensure quality work*], • Would you please [*help me understand what the priorities are*]?	• When you do [*ask me to attend all your team meetings*], • I feel [*tired*]. • My need is [*efficiency because I also supervise five other teams*], • Would you please [*invite me only if there are significant changes*]?

Do it yourself!

Nobody cares here!

You're a bureaucrat...

Lack of context	Motivation	Rules and procedures

Lack of context

- When you do [*ask me to save their project*],
- I feel [*panicked because I already have a lot on my plate*].
- My need is [*clarity*],
- Would you please [*help me understand the big picture*]?

Motivation

- When you do [*tell me that my project is abruptly abandoned*],
- I feel [*sad*].
- My need is [*to do meaningful work*],
- Would you please [*help me understand what motivates your decision*]?

Rules and procedures

- When you do [*ask me to respect time-consuming procedures*],
- I feel [*exhausted because I seriously lack time*].
- My need is [*efficacy*],
- Would you please [*help me understand why this is so important*]?

Pro Tips

When to involve third parties?

If conflict gets worse, involving a third party might be the best option to move forward. Third parties can act as mediators; their neutral and external position might help identify better steps to resolve the conflict.

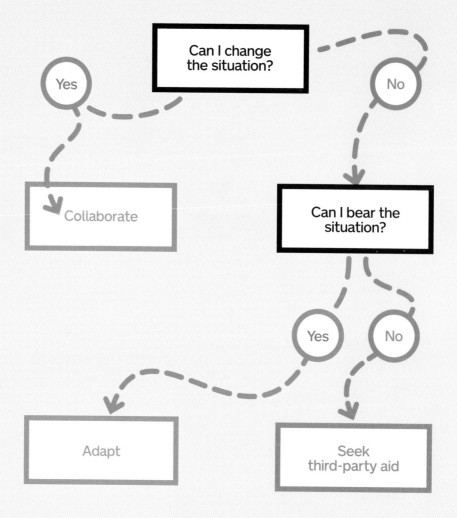

Adapted from Kahane (2017).

NVC to help improve our inner dialogue

The use of NVC can help improve the quality of our internal dialogue by softening our self-judgments, finding a better narrative, and moving forward.

For example:
"I did such a bad job negotiating my salary when I came in."

Nonviolent statement:
1. When I [*find out that I have the lowest salary of the team*],
2. I feel [*frustrated*].
3. My need is [*that my skills are recognized and equally rewarded*],
4. I will [*allow myself enough time to pre-pare and negotiate a salary increase with solid arguments*].

Nonviolent communication to deal with unwanted relationships

Undesired relationships are relationships we maintain out of need more than desire. From goal interference to incompatible personali-ties, we would terminate those relationships rapidly if given a choice. Use nonviolent communication as a first step to release pressure and preserve your mental health.

Origins of the Nonviolent Requests Guide

A Revolutionary Approach to Nonviolent Interactions

Marshall Rosenberg (1934–2015) was an American psychologist who explored the causes of and what could be done to reduce violence. He observed that when we lack the emotional skills to describe our discontent, we tend to issue unproductive judgments and criticisms (called "evaluations" in NVC) perceived as an attack by the other. We might say, for example: "You lied to me" or "You're not accountable," both perceived as an attack, when what we really want to express is: "I am disappointed because you promised you would deliver this work today."

Rosenberg developed and used NVC to improve mediation and communication skills in public schools during the 1960s. He later founded the Center for Nonviolent Communication in 1984, an international peacemaking organization providing NVC training and support in over 60 countries across the world. To learn more about this powerful framework, go to the website for the Center for Nonviolent Communication, www.cnvc.org

List of feelings and needs © 2005 by Center for Nonviolent Communication

Feelings When Your Needs Are Not Satisfied

Afraid
apprehensive
dread
foreboding
frightened
mistrustful
panicked
petrified
scared
suspicious
terrified
wary
worried

Angry
enraged
furious
incensed
indignant
irate
livid
outraged
resentful

Annoyed
aggravated
dismayed
disgruntled
displeased
exasperated
frustrated
impatient
irritated
irked

Aversion
animosity
appalled
contempt
disgusted
dislike
hate
horrified
hostile
repulsed

Confused
ambivalent
baffled
bewildered
dazed
hesitant
lost
mystified
perplexed
puzzled
torn

Disconnected
alienated
aloof
apathetic
bored
cold
detached
distant
distracted
indifferent
numb
removed
uninterested
withdrawn

Disquiet
agitated
alarmed
discombobu-
lated
disconcerted
disturbed
perturbed
rattled
restless
shocked
startled
surprised
troubled
turbulent
turmoil
uncomfortable
uneasy
unnerved
unsettled
upset

Embarrassed
ashamed
chagrined
flustered
guilty
mortified
self-conscious

Fatigue
beat
burned out
depleted
exhausted
lethargic
listless

sleepy
tired
weary
worn out

Pain
agony
anguished
bereaved
devastated
grief
heartbroken
hurt
lonely
miserable
regretful
remorseful

Sad
depressed
dejected
despair
despondent
disappointed
discouraged
disheartened
forlorn
gloomy
heavy-hearted
hopeless
melancholy
unhappy
wretched

Tense
anxious
cranky
distressed
distraught
edgy
fidgety
frazzled
irritable
jittery
nervous
overwhelmed
restless
stressed out

Vulnerable
fragile
guarded
helpless
insecure
leery
reserved
sensitive
shaky

Yearning
envious
jealous
longing
nostalgic
pining
wistful

Feelings When Your Needs Are Satisfied

Affectionate
compassionate
friendly
loving
open-hearted
sympathetic
tender
warm

Engaged
absorbed
alert
curious
engrossed
enchanted
entranced
fascinated
interested
intrigued
involved
spellbound
stimulated

Hopeful
expectant
encouraged
optimistic

Confident
empowered
open
proud
safe
secure

Excited
amazed
animated
ardent
aroused
astonished
dazzled
eager
energetic
enthusiastic
giddy
invigorated
lively
passionate
surprised
vibrant

Grateful
appreciative
moved
thankful
touched

Inspired
amazed
awed
wonder

Joyful
amused
delighted
glad
happy
jubilant
pleased
tickled

Exhilarated
blissful
ecstatic
elated
enthralled
exuberant
radiant
rapturous
thrilled

Peaceful
calm
clear-headed
comfortable
centered
content
equanimous
fulfilled
mellow
quiet
relaxed
relieved
satisfied
serene
still
tranquil
trusting

Refreshed
enlivened
rejuvenated
renewed
rested
restored
revived

Inventory of Needs

Connection
acceptance
affection
appreciation
belonging
cooperation
communication
closeness
community
companionship
compassion
consideration
consistency
empathy
inclusion
intimacy
love
mutuality
nurturing
respect/
self-respect
safety
security
stability
support
to know and be
known
to see and be
seen
to understand
and be
understood
trust
warmth

**Physical
Well-Being**
air
food
movement/
exercise
rest/sleep
safety
shelter
touch
water

Honesty
authenticity
integrity
presence

Play
joy
humor

Peace
beauty
communion
ease
equality
harmony
inspiration
order

Autonomy
choice
freedom
independence
space
spontaneity

Meaning
awareness
celebration
of life
challenge
clarity
competence
consciousness
contribution
creativity
discovery
efficacy
effectiveness
growth
hope
learning
mourning
participation
purpose
self-expression
stimulation
to matter
understanding

Dive Deeper

Discover the science behind the tools and the book

Overview

The tools presented in this book are
the result of an <u>interdisciplinary</u> work.
Find out what body of <u>academic
research</u> lies behind each <u>tool.</u>

4.1
Mutual Understanding and Common Ground

What psycholinguistics reveals about how we understand each other.

4.2
Trust and Psychological Safety

Dive deeper into Amy Edmondson's work.

4.3
Relationship Types

The evolutionary anthropology perspective.

4.4
Face and Politeness

Face theory and the two key needs of mutual consideration.

The Science
Behind
the Tools

All the tools have been designed using a Lean UX cycle at the intersection of current management problems and possible conceptual solutions from social sciences, including psycholinguistics, evolutionary anthropology, and psychology. Translating theoretical concepts into actionable tools has required dozens of iterations and prototypes and chances are the tools will evolve further in the future.

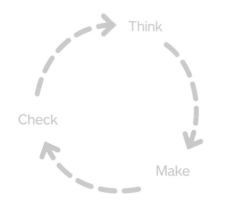

Lean UX Cycle

The Team Alignment Map

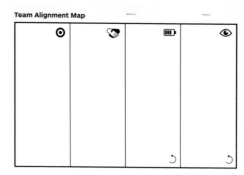

The Team Contract

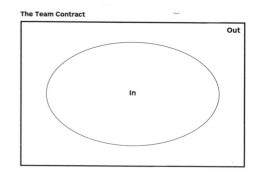

Mutual Understanding and Common Ground
(in Psycholinguistics), p. 264

Relationship Types
(in Evolutionary Anthropology), p. 274

Trust and Psychological Safety
(in Psychology), p. 266

The Fact Finder

The Fact Finder

Assumptions

Limitations

Complete Facts

Generalizations

Judgements

The Respect Card

The Respect Card

Need to be respected
Demonstrate Respect

Need to be valued
Demonstrate Recognition

The Nonviolent Requests Guide

The Nonviolent Requests Guide

When you do
_____
OBSERVATION

I feel
_____
FEELING

My need is
_____
NEED

Would you please
_____ ?
REQUEST

Face and Politeness
(in Psycholinguistics), p. 282

Nonviolent Communication
(in Psychology), p. 242

4.1
Mutual Understanding and Common Ground

What psycholinguistics reveals about how we understand each other.

What Is a Team's Common Ground?

Simply put, common ground is what every team member knows that the other team members know. The mechanics of common ground, common knowledge, shared or mutual understanding and so on, have been described by psycholinguist Herbert Clark and further developed psychologist Steven Pinker. People use language to coordinate joint activities. Team members are mutually dependent, as they need each other to be successful when working together. This interdependence forces everyone to solve coordination problems as everyone needs to constantly align his or her contribution with the contributions of others. As described by Clark, team members need to establish and maintain a sufficient level of common ground to carry out joint activities: a set of knowledge, beliefs, and suppositions shared by all. This matters for interpredictability reasons: team members must be able to successfully predict each others' actions and behaviors to coordinate and achieve what they intend to achieve as a team. How is a team's common ground created and maintained? Through language use and communication. From a Clarkian perspective, this is the raison d'être of communication — to put in place a device to create common ground

and help us coordinate with one another. When there is enough common ground, team members can predict one another's actions successfully and run into less coordination surprises. In other words, they experience less execution problems because their individual contributions are aligned. Coordination surprises occur each time team members see others do things that don't make sense in terms of their own beliefs. As noted by Klein (2005), these originate in common ground breakdowns, i.e. when there is confusion about what's going on and who does what — in other words, who knows what. Project failure factors such as incomplete requirements, lack of user involvement, unrealistic expectations, lack of support, or changing requirements can be interpreted as symptoms of common ground breakdowns, highlighting the importance of creating and maintaining enough common ground, common knowledge, or mutual understanding to ensure successful teamwork.

Successful Teamwork

Effective Coordination

Relevant Common Ground

Successful Conversations

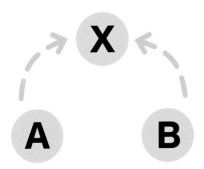

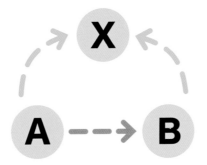

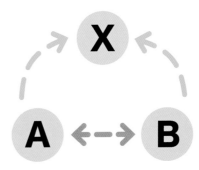

Private Knowledge

All know something, but don't know that the others know too.

- A knows X
- B knows X

Example

- Ann knows that there is a man walking in the street
- Bob knows that there is a man walking in the street
- Ann doesn't know that Bob knows it
- Bob doesn't know that Ann knows it

Shared Knowledge

All know something, but only some know that the others know.

- A knows X
- B knows X
- A knows that B knows X
- B doesn't know that A knows X

Example

- Ann knows that there is a man walking in the street
- Bob knows that there is a man walking in the street
- Ann knows that Bob knows it
- Bob doesn't know that Ann knows it

Common Ground, Common Knowledge, or Mutual Understanding

All know something, and also know that all the others know.

- A knows X
- B knows X
- A and B know that they both know X

Example

- Ann knows that there is a man walking in the street
- Bob knows that there is a man walking in the street
- Ann and Bob both know that they both know it

J. De Freitas, K. Thomas, P. DeScioli, and S. Pinker, "Common Knowledge, Coordination, and Strategic Mentalizing in Human Social Life," Proceedings of the National Academy of Sciences 116, no. 28 (2019): 13751–13758.

Building Up Common Ground

Common ground accumulates as the result of a social and cognitive process described as the "grounding process" by Herb Clark. This process allows two or more people to create and validate mutual understanding by signaling each other (1) that evidence of understanding is reached or (2) that misunderstanding is in the air and that further iterations are needed to be successful.

1
Signaling Understanding

Mutual understanding is achieved when people signal, verbally or nonverbally, signs of positive evidence of understanding. In a conversation, positive signals include:
- Nodding: "uh-huh," "I see," "Mmm"
- Continuing: continuing the sentence of the other
- Answering: answering a question
- Examplifying: giving an example of what has just been said

This process of grounding unfolds in three co-occurring activities or levels that happen at the same time. Speakers and listeners must climb together a virtual ladder in this sequence:

1. **Attending**: speakers make sounds and gestures and listeners must attend to these sounds and gestures.
2. **Perceiving**: speakers must formulate messages with these sounds and gestures and listeners must identify those messages.
3. **Understanding**: speakers must mean something with these messages and listeners must make the right inferences to understand their meaning.

2
Signaling Misunderstanding

When things are unclear, the following signals illustrate misunderstanding, or negative evidence of understanding:
- Hesitating: "uh"
- Reformulating: "If I understand …," "You mean…," etc.
- Clarifying: ask good clarification questions, using the Fact Finder for example.

These repair mechanisms create new opportunities to build mutual understanding.

+
Ask. Listen. Repeat.
A simple method to boost mutual understanding is to validate our own understanding by repeating what the other person just told us.

The Grounding Process

Speaking and listening are themselves a joint activity, like dancing a waltz or playing a piano duet. The active participation of both parties is needed at each step to create common ground successfully.

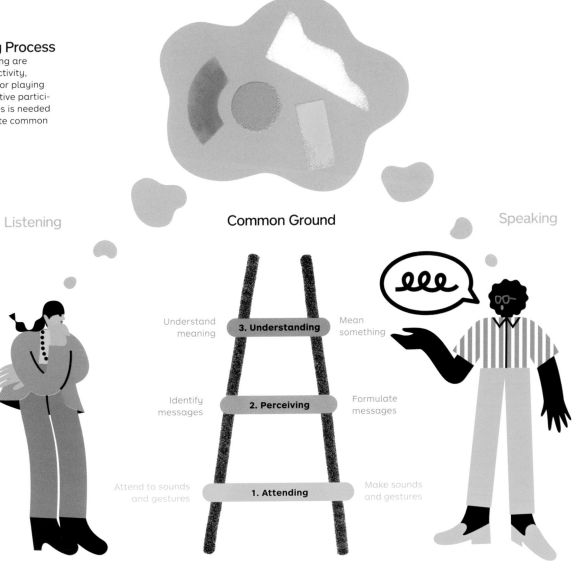

Listening

Common Ground

Speaking

Understand meaning — **3. Understanding** — Mean something

Identify messages — **2. Perceiving** — Formulate messages

Attend to sounds and gestures — **1. Attending** — Make sounds and gestures

Impact of Communication Channels on Common Ground Creation

Not all communication channels have the same impact on common ground creation (Clark and Brennan, 1991). Face-to-face conversation remains the most effective technology followed by videoconferencing, which makes great progress in lowering the distance barrier and developing immersive experiences. Co-located task forces, war rooms, and crisis units still illustrate the importance of in-person meetings to create common knowledge rapidly when people need to be extremely effective.

All the other communication channels present communication obstacles compared to face-to-face interaction—for example, the lack of nonverbal and contextual infor-mation, bad signal, delays, or the inability to get an immediate explanation when receiving an ambiguous email. These obsta-cles can considerably reduce our ability to build common ground and coordinate as a team.

Synchronous Communication

Prefer face-to-face, video-conference, and conference calls when the team's common ground needs a strong boost, for example when:

- Initiating new activities and projects
- Solving problems
- Performing creative tasks

Asynchronous Communication

Use email, chat rooms, and other asynchronous media for incremental updates such as:

- Notifying of changes
- Co-editing documents
- Sharing updates
- Status reports

Communication Effectiveness
of Various Media Types

*Adapted from Media Richness Theory,
https://en.wikipedia.org/wiki/Media_
richness_theory*

Face-to-face conversation	Video conversation	Telephone conversation	Addressed letters, emails, reports	Short messages	Unaddressed spam, posters

4.2
Trust and Psychological Safety

Dive deeper into Amy Edmondson's work.

What Is Psychological Safety and How Does It Help Teams Perform Better?

According to Amy Edmondson, psychological safety is "the belief that the team is safe for interpersonal risk taking. That one will not be punished or humiliated for speaking up with ideas, questions, concerns, or mistakes." When the climate is psychologically safe, team members are not afraid to speak up; they engage in a productive dialogue that fosters the proactive learning behaviors required to understand the environment, the clients, and solve problems together effectively.

Solving complex problems is the bread and butter of any cutting-edge business, where constant experimentation is required: intense phases of trial and error until teams get things right, which by definition is the very basis of business innovation. Faced with uncertainty, psychologically safe teams are propelled into a performance spiral, where making mistakes is not considered a failure, but rather as experimentation and a learning opportunity. Creating safety is not about being nice to each other or reducing performance standards, but rather about creating a culture of openness where teammates can share learnings, be direct, take risks, admit they "screwed up," and are willing to ask for help when they're in over their head.

In Google's top-performing teams, people feel safe to speak up, collaborate, and experiment together. A large internal study conducted by their HR teams highlighted psychological safety as the key enabler of high-performance teamwork.

In a world characterized by Volatility, Uncertainty, Complexity, and Ambiguity (VUCA), creating and maintaining a psychologically safe climate must become a managerial priority for those who want to keep up in the global competitive race.

As noted by Edmondson, psychological safety is not about being nice or compromising performance standards. Conflict arises in every team, but psychological safety makes it possible to channel that energy into productive interactions, that is, constructive disagreement, an open exchange of ideas, and learning from different points of view. Similarly, psychological safety is not about creating a comfortable climate by relaxing performance standards and making people feel unaccountable at the individual level. Psychological safety and performance standards are two separate, equally important dimensions, and both are needed to achieve superior team performance (Edmondson 2018).

A. C. Edmondson, The Fearless Organization: Creating Psychological Safety in the Workplace for Learning, Innovation, and Growth *(John Wiley & Sons, 2018).*

Psychological Safety and Business Performance

Both high psychological safety and high performance standards are needed to enter the learning zone and achieve superior team performance.

Adapted from Amy Edmondson.

Comfort Zone
Team members enjoy working together but are not challenged by work and don't see compelling reasons to engage in additional challenges.

Learning Zone
Everyone can collaborate, learn from each other, and get complex, innovative work done.

Apathy Zone
People are physically present but their mind is elsewhere. Significant energy is poured into making each other's life miserable.

Anxiety Zone
Maybe the worst area to work in, people must meet high standards and expectations mostly on their own, because they are suspicious and experience anxiety toward their colleagues.

Psychological Safety

Performance Standards

How to Rapidly Assess Psychological Safety

These seven questions help identify what works well and areas needing improvement. We recommend that this assessment be done between colleagues of the same hierarchical level to avoid biased responses.

1 Respond individually

Take two minutes individually to answer
the seven questions and calculate your personal score.

2 Share the personal scores

Share the personal scores with your colleagues.

3 Discuss and investigate the gaps

Enter an open discussion to understand the different
perceptions, question by question.

4 Agree on possible actions

If areas for improvement are identified, agree on appropriate solutions. The four add-ons presented on the
next page can help.

		Strongly Disagree	Disagree	Somewhat Disagree	Neutral	Somewhat Agree	Agree	Strongly Agree	Your Scores
1 Learn from mistakes	If you make a mistake on this team, it is often held against you.	7	6	5	4	3	2	1	
2 Productive conflict	Members of this team are able to bring up problems and tough issues.	1	2	3	4	5	6	7	
3 Gain from diversity	People on this team sometimes reject others for being different.	7	6	5	4	3	2	1	
4 Foster exploration	It is safe to take a risk on this team.	1	2	3	4	5	6	7	
5 Mutual assistance	It is difficult to ask other members of this team for help.	7	6	5	4	3	2	1	
6 Strong partnership	No one on this team would deliberately act in a way that undermines my efforts.	1	2	3	4	5	6	7	
7 Optimal contributions	Working with members of this team, my unique skills and talents are valued and utilized.	1	2	3	4	5	6	7	

Total

+
As a rule of thumb, 40 and above can be considered a good total score.

Adapted from Amy Edmondson, 1999.

Differences Between Trust, Psychological Safety, and Similar Concepts

Psychological Safety

The belief held by members of a team that the team is safe for interpersonal risk taking, that one will not be punished or humiliated for speaking up with ideas, questions, concerns, or mistakes (Edmondson 1999).

Psychological safety describes a team climate and is experienced at the group level (Edmondson 2018); it captures the extent to which one believes that others will give them the benefit of the doubt when taking risks (Edmondson 2004). It involves but goes beyond trust.

Adapted from Frazier et al. (2017).

Empowerment

The motivational state employees feel when they have a sense of control over their work (Spreitzer 1995).

Engagement

The cognitive state describing individuals who invest their personal resources and energies into their work roles and tasks (Christian, Garza, and Slaughter 2011; Kahn 1990).

Trust

The willingness to be vulnerable to the actions of others (Mayer, Davis, and Schoorman 1995).

Trust is experienced at the interaction level, between two individuals. One might trust one colleague and not the other (Edmondson 2019).

4.3
Relationship Types

The evolutionary anthropology perspective.

Relationships:
The Four Playing Modes

When we work as a team we don't just work; we also manage our relationships with our colleagues. We constantly seek, make, sustain, repair, adjust, judge, construe, and sanction relationships. The anthropologist Alan Fiske brilliantly identified the "grammar" of human relationships in the form of four elementary types of bonds called relationship types. These four playing modes each organize a way of distributing resources between participants (adapted from Fiske 1992 and Pinker 2008).

The four modes are:

1. **Share**: "What's mine is yours, and vice versa." People are driven by a sense of belonging and decisions are made by consensus. Typical of communities such as couples, close friends, or allies.
2. **Authority**: "Who's in charge?" People are driven by power, rules and decisions are authoritative; one person is positioned above (gaining prestige) and the other is positioned below (gaining protection). Typical in hierarchical structures such as bosses and subordinates, soldiers and commanders, or professors and students.
3. **Reciprocate**: "To each the same." People are driven by equality, giving and taking in the same quantity, and decisions are made by voting (one person, one vote). Typical in peer groups such as clubs, carpools, and acquaintances: getting and giving presents, being invited and inviting in return, and so on.
4. **Bargain**: "To each in due proportion." People are driven by achievements; transactions are based on elements such as perceived utility, individual performance, and market price. Typical in for-profit businesses, stock markets, buyer and seller relationships.

What Fiske reveals is that when the two parties play in the same mode, things go pretty well. But if one plays in one mode and one in another — when there is a mode mismatch — things go wrong. To add more complexity, we never interact with one another using just one playing mode. We constantly switch modes depending on the context and the task at hand. The challenge is to navigate together successfully through the playing mode changes because the rules of the game change in each mode.

A. P. Fiske, "The Four Elementary Forms of Sociality: Framework for a Unified Theory of Social Relations," Psychological Review 99, no. 4 (1992): 689.
S. Pinker, M. A. Nowak,and J. J. Lee, "The Logic of Indirect Speech," Proceedings of the National Academy of Sciences 105, no. 3 (2008): 833–838.

+

What is your team's main playing mode, in what situation?
Understanding and aligning playing modes helps minimize unintentional gaffes; in each playing mode the rules of the game change and so do the expected behaviors.

Teamwork
Expectations

Playing Mode	**Share** *What's mine is yours*	**Authority** *Who's in charge?*	**Reciprocate** *Give and take*	**Bargain** *Pay in due proportion*
Appears in children by	Infancy	Age of 3	Age of 4	Age of 9
Primary motivation	Belonging • intimacy • altruism • generosity • kindness • caring	Belonging • power vs. protection • status, recognition vs. obedience, loyalty	Equality • equal treatment • strict fairness	Achievement • utility • benefits • profits
Examples	Families, close friends, clubs, ethnic groups, social movements, open-source communities	Subordinates and their bosses, soldiers and commanders, professors and students	Roommates (errands, rounds of beers), carpools, acquaintances (getting and giving presents, dinner parties, birthdays)	The business world: buyer and seller, get the best deal, make a profit, negotiate a contract, receive dividends
Organization	Community	Hierarchical	Peer group	Rationally structured
Contribution from members	Everyone contributes according to their personal abilities	Supervisors direct and control the work	Everyone does the same or equivalent work	Work is divided based on performance and productivity
Decision-making process	Consensus	Chain of authority	Voting, drawing lots	Arguments
Resource ownership	Owned by all, no bookkeeping	Increases with the hierarchical level	Divided in equal parts	In proportion to the contribution or the invested capital
Rewards	Common pool for rewards, no individual compensation	By rank and seniority	Same reward of same amount for everyone	By market value and individual performance

Crossing Playing Modes: Not a Good Idea

Emotions can run high when we assume that others are playing in the same mode we are, when in fact they aren't. The behaviors perceived as appropriate in one mode can be perceived as completely inappropriate in another one. Everyone is doing their best, but people offend each other involuntarily simply because they are operating in a different mode. That creates situations where the parties feel embarrassment, taboo, or even feel immoral (Pinker 2007).

Aligned Modes

A close friend
(Share = Share)

Take food from the plate of...

Misaligned Modes

A superior
(Share ≠ Authority)

S. Pinker, The Stuff of Thought: Language as a Window into Human Nature *(Penguin, 2007).*

A client
(Bargain = Bargain)

At a restaurant
(Bargain = Bargain)

Make a profit from a sale to...

Pay for your dinner...

A parent
(Bargain ≠ Share)

At your parents' house
(Bargain ≠ Share)

In teams, misaligned playing modes create awkward situations, can damage relationships, and can turn into conflict.

As an experienced professional, Tati tries to direct others, while they assume everyone should have an equal say.
(Authority ≠ Reciprocate)

The team is waiting for Antonio's directions, while he assumes he doesn't have to take responsibility because he's not being paid for that.
(Authority ≠ Bargain)

Susan thinks Ann is the most competent person to meet a client with her. Others think it's a matter of taking turns.
(Bargain ≠ Reciprocate)

Aligned Playing Modes: Crucial for Family Businesses

The risk of conflict is high in family businesses. Collaborating with family members in a business context creates a highly complex relational setting.

In a family business system, members often cumulate several roles (family member, owner, manager), which imply different value systems and interests. The more roles family members accumulate, the greater the likelihood of crossing the boundaries of each role and experience a playing mode mismatch with the other family members. Large family businesses address this challenge by designing their own family governance model to clarify the expectations and structure the responsibilities of each role. These are often compiled in a so-called family constitution, a document that formalizes the relationships in the family, thus minimizing unnecessary conflict due to the crossing of types.

Keywords: family business, family governance, family constitution

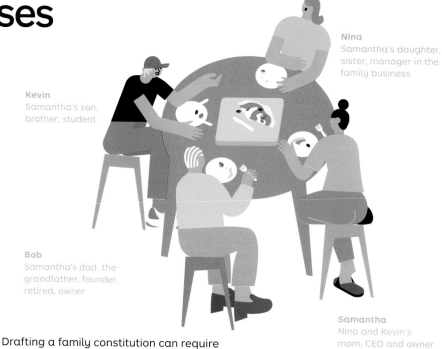

Kevin
Samantha's son, brother, student

Nina
Samantha's daughter, sister, manager in the family business

Bob
Samantha's dad, the grandfather, founder, retired, owner

Samantha
Nina and Kevin's mom, CEO and owner

Drafting a family constitution can require substantial effort, skills, and external resources. To preserve harmony, smaller family-owned businesses like shops, restaurants, and craft businesses can as a first step establish a Team Contract to define some basic rules of the game in the different roles.

Family Roles Overlap
as a Source of Conflict

Bob (Share) — **Samantha** (Authority)
Despite a year of exceptional results,
Bob keeps giving lengthy advice to
Samantha on what he would have done
in her place.

Kevin (Share) — **Samantha** (Bargain)
Kevin's upset because his sister Nina
won't let him use her company car to
go to a party.

Kevin (Reciprocate) — **Samantha** (Bargain)
Kevin is even angrier when he finds out that
his sister got a financial bonus at work while
he doesn't have enough pocket money.

Nina (Bargain) — **Samantha** (Authority)
Nina is angry at her mother because
she promoted another person to a position
she wanted.

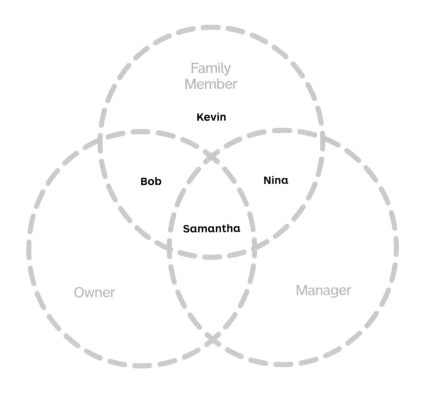

Source of the Three-Circle Model: R. Tagiuri and J. Davis, "Bivalent Attributes of the Family Firm,"
Family Business Review 9, no. 2 (Summer 1996), p. 200.

4.4
Face and Politeness

Face theory and two key needs of mutual consideration.

Politeness:
Our Two Key Social Needs

The anthropologists Penelope Brown and Stephen Levinson provided a unique description of mutual consideration in their book *Politeness: Some Universals in Language Usage*. They have developed a groundbreaking theory of politeness based on the concept of "face", from the expression "losing face" described by the sociologist Erving Goffmann as the positive social value that a person claims for him- or herself.

For Brown and Levinson, demonstrating consideration and being polite means doing "facework" by actively taking care of the face of each other. That is achieved by addressing two universally shared "social needs" (Brown and Levinson 1987):

- The need to be approved, or valued: when the actions and behaviors of others reflect a positive image of ourselves. That happens when we are thanked, expressed sympathy toward, recognized, and so forth, and it doesn't happen when we are ignored, disapproved of, or embarrassed in public.
- The need to be autonomous, or respected: the need to protect our freedom of action, not being impeded or trapped by others, that our private territory is not invaded. That happens when we are asked for permission to be interrupted, when we receive apologies in advance for an inconvenience, or when honorific titles such as Mrs., Mr., Dr., Prof., and so on are used to showcase our social status. That doesn't happen when we are prevented from having our morning coffee to hear complaints, when things are imposed on us, or when we receive warnings and summonses.

These (almost) antagonistic needs illustrate, according to psychologist Steven Pinker, the duality of social life: connection and autonomy, intimacy and power, solidarity and status. If I do whatever I want, my need to be respected is satisfied but I might not be valued by others. Wanting to be valued and respected constitutes our social DNA (Fiske, 1992) and we become very picky when these are threatened. Demonstrating mutual consideration, in Brown and Levinson's view, consists of doing what's right: choosing the right words and expressions to minimize the risk of making each other lose face. In other words, to be polite.

Search keywords: politeness theory, Brown and Levinson, theory of the strategic speaker, Steven Pinker, politeness

We value people who show us consideration by respecting our two social needs. We are less appreciative of those who don't. The same is true for the others.

Social need to be respected
Congratulations!

Social need to be valued
May I ask you to follow me?

What Is a Fair Process?

Valuing and respecting each other are the two key pillars of fairness. Fairness is a crucial foundation on which to grow teams and implement any diversity, equity, and inclusion initiative.

Implementing a fair process in a team or in an organization consists of making decisions so that everyone's needs to be valued and respected are equitably addressed. As illustrated by INSEAD's Cham Kim and Renée Mauborgne, this is achieved by adopting the three high-level principles of:

1. Engagement
2. Explanation
3. Expectation clarity

Research shows that people accept compromise and even sacrifice their personal interests when they believe that the process leading to important decisions and results is fair. Despite the evidence, some managers struggle to adopt a fair process approach because they fear their authority will be questioned and their power will decrease, which reveals a misunderstanding of the process: a fair process is not decision by consensus, or democracy in the workplace. Its goal is to nurture and pursue the best ideas.

The Three Principles of a Fair (Decision) Process

1
Engagement
Involving individuals in decisions by inviting their input and encouraging them to challenge one another's ideas.

Supported by:
- The Team Alignment Map
- The Team Contract

2
Explanation
Clarifying the thinking behind a final decision.

Supported by:
- The Team Alignment Map
- The Team Contract

3
Expectation Clarity
Stating the new rules of the game, including performance standards, penalties for failure, and new responsibilities.

Supported by:
- The Team Contract

Source: W. Kim and R. Mauborgne, "Fair Process," Harvard Business Review 75 (1997): 65–75.

Templates

Download the templates on teamalignment.co/downloads

Team Alignment Map

Mission: *Period:*

Joint Objectives ⊙	Joint Commitments 🤝	Joint Resources 🔋	Joint Risks 👁
What do we intend to achieve together?	Who does what and with whom?	What resources do we need?	What can prevent us from succeeding?

ʘStrategyzer

Team Alignment Map

Mission: *Period:*

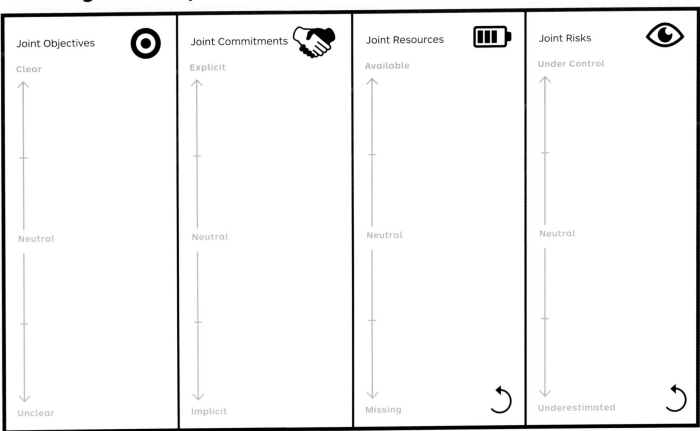

Joint Objectives	Joint Commitments	Joint Resources	Joint Risks
Clear	Explicit	Available	Under Control
Neutral	Neutral	Neutral	Neutral
Unclear	Implicit	Missing	Underestimated

Ⓤ Strategyzer

The Team Contract

What are the rules and behaviors that we want to abide by in our team?
As individuals, do we have preferences for working in a certain way?

Team:

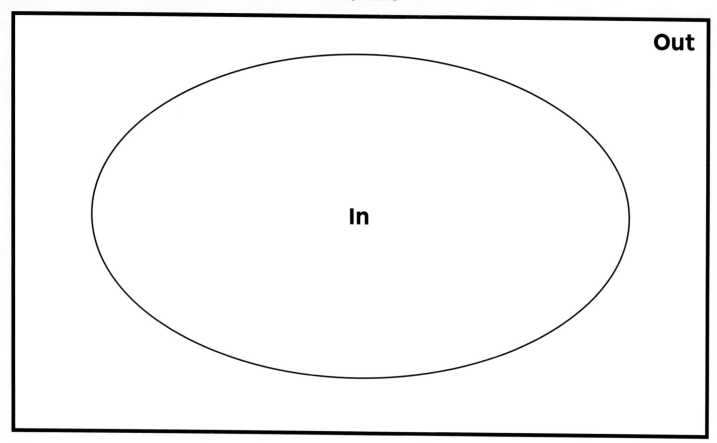

Out

In

Ⓢ Strategyzer

The Fact Finder

Assumptions
Creative interpretations,
hypotheses, or predictions

HEAR	ASK
"He/she thinks..."	What makes you recognize that...?
"He/she believes..."	How do you know...?
"He/she doesn't/should..."	What evidence shows that...?
"He/she likes..."	What makes you think so?
"You/they/... will..."	
"Business/life/love/... will..."	

Limitations
Imaginary restrictions and obligations
that narrow down options

HEAR	ASK
"I must..."	What might happen if...?
"We have to"	What's preventing
"I can't..."	you/us from...?
"I don't..."	
"We shouldn't..."	

Incomplete Facts or Experiences
Lack of precision in the description

HEAR	Complete Facts	ASK
"I heard..."		Who? What?
"They said..."		When? Where?
"She saw..."		How? How many?
"I feel..."		Could you be more precise?
		What do you mean by...?

First-Order Reality
*Physically observable qualities
of a thing or situation*

Generalizations
Turning a particular into
a universal case

HEAR	ASK
"Always"	Always?
"Never"	Never?
"Nobody"	Nobody?
"Everyone"	Everyone?
"People"	People?
	Are you sure?

Judgments
Subjective assessment of
a thing, a situation, or a person

HEAR	ASK
"I am..."	What tells you...?
"Life is..."	How is this manifested?
"It's good/bad to..."	In what way is this unacceptable?
"It's important to..."	Something on your mind?
"It's easy/difficult to..."	

Second-Order Reality
*Perceptions, personal interpretations
of the first-order reality*

Strategyzer

The Respect Card
Tips for tactful communication.

Need to be respected
Demonstrate Respect

Questioning rather than commanding
Will you...?

Express doubt
I don't suppose you might...?

Hedge the request
..., if possible.

Acknowledge the impingement
I'm sure you're busy, but...

Indicate reluctance
I normally wouldn't ask, but...

Apologize
I'm sorry to bother you, but...

Acknowledge a debt
I'd be grateful if you would...

Use honorifics
Mr., Mrs., Miss, Professor, Dr., etc...

Be indirect
I'm looking for a pen.

Request forgiveness
You must forgive me but...
Could I borrow your pen?

Minimize request
I just wanted to ask you if I could use your pen.

Pluralize the person responsible
*We forgot to tell you that you needed
to buy your plane ticket by yesterday.*

Hesitate
Can I, uh,...?

Impersonalize
Smoking is not permitted.

Need to be valued
Demonstrate Recognition

Thank
A big thank you.

Wish
Be well, have a nice day.

Inquire
How are you? How is it going?

Compliment
Nice sweater.

Anticipate
You must be hungry.

Advice
Take care.

Endear
My friend, mate, buddy, pal, honey, dear, bro, guys.

Solicit agreement
You know?

Attend to others
*You must be hungry, it's been a long
time since breakfast. How about some lunch?*

Avoid disagreement
*A: You don't like it?
B: Yes, yes I like it, um, I usually don't eat this but it's good.*

Assume agreement
So, when are you coming to see us?

Hedge opinion
You really should sort of try harder

RISKY BEHAVIORS
Direct orders
Interrupt
Give warnings
Prohibit
Threaten
Suggestions
Reminders
Advice

RISKY BEHAVIORS
Embarrass
Disapprove
Ignore
Openly criticize
Contempt, ridicule
Speak only about yourself
Mention taboo topics
Insults, accusations, complaints

⊕Strategyzer

The Nonviolent Requests Guide

Feelings *negative feelings when your needs are not satisfied*

AFRAID	CONFUSED	EMBARRASSED	SAD
apprehensive	ambivalent	ashamed	depressed
dread	baffled	chagrined	dejected
foreboding	bewildered	flustered	despair
frightened	dazed	guilty	despondent
mistrustful	hesitant	mortified	disappointed
panicked	lost	self-conscious	discouraged
petrified	mystified		disheartened
scared	perplexed	**TENSE**	forlorn
suspicious	puzzled	anxious	gloomy
terrified	torn	cranky	heavy hearted
wary		distressed	hopeless
worried	**DISCONNECTED**	distraught	melancholy
	alienated	edgy	unhappy
ANNOYED	aloof	fidgety	wretched
aggravated	apathetic	frazzled	
dismayed	bored	irritable	**VULNERABLE**
disgruntled	cold	jittery	fragile
displeased	detached	nervous	guarded
exasperated	indifferent	overwhelmed	helpless
frustrated	numb	restless	insecure
impatient	removed	stressed out	leery
irritated	uninterested		reserved
irked	withdrawn	**PAIN**	sensitive
		agony	
ANGRY	**DISQUIET**	anguished	**YEARNING**
enraged	agitated	bereaved	envious
furious	alarmed	devastated	jealous
incensed	disconcerted	grief	longing
indignant	disturbed	heartbroken	nostalgic
irate	perturbed	hurt	pining
livid	rattled	lonely	wistful
outraged	restless	miserable	
resentful	shocked	regretful	
	startled	remorseful	
	surprised		
AVERSION	troubled	**FATIGUE**	
animosity	turbulent	beat	
appalled	turmoil	burnt out	
contempt	uncomfortable	depleted	
disgusted	uneasy	exhausted	
dislike	unnerved	lethargic	
hate	unsettled	listless	
horrified	upset	sleepy	
hostile		tired	
repulsed		weary	
		worn out	

When you do

_____

OBSERVATION

I feel

_____

FEELING

My need is

_____

NEED

Would you please

_____ ?

REQUEST

Needs

CONNECTION	PHYSICAL WELL-BEING	AUTONOMY
acceptance	air	choice
affection	food	freedom
appreciation	movement/	independence
belonging	exercise	space
cooperation	rest/sleep	spontaneity
communication	safety	
closeness	shelter	**MEANING**
community	touch	awareness
companionship	water	celebration of
compassion		life
consideration	**HONESTY**	challenge
consistency	authenticity	clarity
empathy	integrity	competence
inclusion	presence	consciousness
intimacy		contribution
love	**PLAY**	creativity
mutuality	joy	discovery
nurturing	humor	efficacy
respect/self-		effectiveness
respect	**PEACE**	growth
safety	beauty	hope
security	communication	learning
stability	ease	mourning
support	equality	participation
to know and	harmony	purpose
be known	inspiration	self-expression
to see and	order	stimulation
be seen		to matter
to understand		understanding
trust		
warmth		

Strategyzer

Afterword

References

Section 1: Discover the
Team Alignment Map

Mission and Period

Deci, E. L., and R. M. Ryan. *(1985). Intrinsic Motivation and Self-Determination in Human Behavior*. Plenum Press.
Edmondson, A. C., and J. F. Harvey. 2017. *Extreme Teaming: Lessons in Complex, Cross-Sector Leadership*. Emerald Group Publishing.
Locke, E. A., and G. P. Latham. 1990. *A Theory of Goal Setting & Task Performance*. Prentice-Hall Inc.

Joint Objectives

Clark, H. H. 1996. *Using Language*. Cambridge University Press.
Klein, H. J., M. J. Wesson, J. R. Hollenbeck, and B. J. Alge. 1999. "Goal Commitment and the Goal-Setting Process: Conceptual Clarification and Empirical Synthesis." *Journal of Applied Psychology* 84 (6): 885.
Lewis, D. K. 1969. *Convention: A Philosophical Study*. Harvard University Press.

Locke, E. A., and G. P. Latham. 1990. *A Theory of Goal Setting & Task Performance*. Prentice-Hall.
Schelling, T. C. 1980. *The Strategy of Conflict*. Harvard University Press.

Joint Commitments

Clark, H. H. 2006. "Social Actions, Social Commitments." In *Roots of Human Sociality: Culture, Cognition and Human Interaction*, edited by Stephen C. Levinson and N. J. Enfield, 126–150. Oxford, UK: Berg Press.
Edmondson, A. C., and J. F. Harvey. 2017. *Extreme Teaming: Lessons in Complex, Cross-Sector Leadership*. Emerald Publishing.
Gilbert, M. 2014. *Joint Commitment: How We Make the Social World*. Oxford University Press.
Schmitt, F. 2004. *Socializing Metaphysics: The Nature of Social Reality*. Rowman & Littlefield.
Tuomela, R., and M. Tuomela. 2003. "Acting as a Group Member and Collective Commitment." *Protosociology* 18: 7–65.

Joint Resources

Corporate Finance Institute® (CFI). n.d. "What Are the Main Types of Assets"? https://corporatefinanceinstitute.com/resources/knowledge/accounting/types-of-assets/

Joint Risks

Aven, T. 2010. "On How to Define, Understand and Describe Risk." *Reliability Engineering & System Safety* 95 (6): 623–631.
Cobb, A. T. 2011. *Leading Project Teams: The Basics of Project Management and Team Leadership*. Sage.
Cohen, P. 2011. "An Approach for Wording Risks." http://www.betterprojects.net/2011/09/approach-for-wording-risks.html.
Lonergan, K. 2015. "Example Project Risks – Good and Bad Practice." https://www.pmis-consulting.com/example-project-risks-goodand-bad-practice.
Mar, A. 2015. "130 Project Risks" (List). https://management.simplicable.com/management/new/130-project-risks.

Power, B. 2014. "Writing Good Risk Statements." *ISACA Journal*. https://www.isaca.org/Journal/archives/2014/Volume-3/Pages/Writing-Good-Risk-Statements.aspx#f1.

Project Management Institute. 2013. *A Guide to the Project Management Body of Knowledge* (PMBOK® Guide). 5th ed.

Assessments

Avdiji, H., D. Elikan, S. Missonier, and Y. Pigneur. 2018. "Designing Tools for Collectively Solving Ill-Structured Problems." In *Proceedings of the 51st Hawaii International Conference on System Sciences* (January), 400–409.

Avdiji, H., S. Missonier, and S. Mastrogiacomo. 2015. "How to Manage IS Team Coordination in Real Time." In *Proceedings of the International Conference on Information Systems* (ICIS) 2015, December 2015, 13–16.

Mastrogiacomo, S., S. Missonier, and R. Bonazzi. 2014. "Talk Before It's Too Late: Reconsidering the Role of Conversation in Information Systems Project Management." *Journal of Management Information Systems* 31 (1): 47–78.

Section 2: Put the Map into Action

Corporate Rebels. "The 8 Trends." https://corporate-rebels.com/trends/.

Kaplan, R. S., and D. P. Norton. 2006. *Alignment: Using the Balanced Scorecard to Create Corporate Synergies*. Harvard Business School Press.

Kniberg, H. 2014. "Spotify Engineering Culture Part 1." Spotify Labs. https://labs.spotify.com/2014/03/27/spotifyengineering-culture-part-1/

Kniberg, H. 2014. "Spotify Engineering Culture Part 2." Spotify Labs. https://labs.spotify.com/2014/09/20/spotifyengineering-culture-part-2/

Larman, C., and B. Vodde. 2016. *Large-Scale Scrum: More with LeSS*. Addison-Wesley.

Leffingwell, D. 2018. SAFe 4.5 *Reference Guide: Scaled Agile Framework for Lean Enterprises*. Addison-Wesley.

Section 3: Trust Among Team Members

Psychological Safety

Christian M. S., A. S. Garza, and J. E. Slaughter. 2011. "Work Engagement: A Quantitative Review and Test of Its Relations with Task and Contextual Performance." *Personnel Psychology* 64: 89–136. http://dx.doi.org/10.1111/j.1744-6570.2010.01203.x

Duhigg, C. 2016. "What Google Learned from Its Quest to Build the Perfect Team." *New York Times Magazine*. February 25.

Edmondson, A. 1999. "Psychological Safety and Learning Behavior in Work Teams." *Administrative Science Quarterly* 44: 350–383. http://dx.doi.org/10.2307/2666999

Edmondson, A. C. 2004. "Psychological Safety, Trust, and Learning in Organizations: A Group-Level Lens." In *Trust and Distrust in Organizations: Dilemmas and Approaches*, edited by R. M. Kramer and K. S. Cook, 239–272. Russell Sage Foundation.

Edmondson, A. C. 2018. *The Fearless Organization: Creating Psychological Safety in the Workplace for Learning, Innovation, and Growth*. John Wiley & Sons.

Edmondson, A. C., and J. F. Harvey. 2017. *Extreme Teaming: Lessons in Complex, Cross-Sector Leadership*. Emerald Publishing.

Frazier, M. L., S. Fainshmidt, R. L. Klinger, A. Pezeshkan, and V. Vracheva. 2017. "Psychological Safety: A Meta-Analytic Review and Extension." *Personnel Psychology* 70 (1): 113–165.

Gallo, P. 2018. *The Compass and the Radar: The Art of Building a Rewarding Career While Remaining True to Yourself*. Bloomsbury Business.

Kahn, W. A. 1990. "Psychological Conditions of Personal Engagement and Disengagement at Work." *Academy of Management Journal* 33: 692–724. http://dx.doi.org/10.2307/256287

Mayer, R. C., J. H. Davis, and F. D. Schoorman. 1995. "An Integrative Model of Organizational Trust." *Academy of Management Review* 20: 709–734. http://dx.doi.org/10.5465/AMR.1995.9508080335

Schein, E. H., and W. G. Benni. 1965. *Personal and Organizational Change Through Group Methods: The Laboratory Approach*. John Wiley & Sons.

Spreitzer, G. M. 1995. "Psychological Empowerment in the Workplace: Dimensions, Measurement, and Validation." *Academy of Management Journal* 38: 1442–1465. doi: 10.2037/256865

The Team Contract

Edmondson, A. C. 2018. *The Fearless Organization: Creating Psychological Safety in the Workplace for Learning, Innovation, and Growth*. John Wiley & Sons.

Fiske, A. P., and P. E. Tetlock. 1997. "Taboo Trade-Offs: Reactions to Transactions That Transgress the Spheres of Justice." *Political Psychology* 18 (2): 255–297.

The Fact Finder

Edmondson, A. C. 2018. *The Fearless Organization: Creating Psychological Safety in the Workplace for Learning, Innovation, and Growth*. John Wiley & Sons.

Kourilsky, F. 2014. *Du désir au plaisir de changer: le coaching du changement*. Dunod.

Watzlawick, P. 1984. *The Invented Reality: Contributions to Constructivism*. W. W. Norton.

Zacharis, P. 2016. *La boussole du langage*. https://www.patrickzacharis.be/la-boussole-du-langage/

The Respect Card

Brown, P., and S. C. Levinson. 1987. *Politeness: Some Universals in Language Usage*. Vol. 4. Cambridge University Press.

Culpeper, J. 2011. "Politeness and Impoliteness." In *Pragmatics of Society*, edited by W. Bublitz, A. H. Jucker, and K. P. Schneider. Vol. 5, 393. Mouton de Gruyter.

Fiske, A. P. 1992. "The Four Elementary Forms of Sociality: Framework for a Unified Theory of Social Relations." *Psychological Review* 99 (4): 689.

Lee, J. J., and S. Pinker. 2010. "Rationales for Indirect Speech: The Theory of the Strategic Speaker." *Psychological Review* 117 (3): 785.

Locher, M. A., and R. J. Watts. 2008. "Relational Work and Impoliteness: Negotiating Norms of Linguistic Behaviour." In *Impoliteness in Language*. Studies on its Interplay with Power in Theory and Practice, edited by D. Bousfield and M. A. Locher, 77-99. Mouton de Gruyter.

Pinker, S. 2007. *The Stuff of Thought: Language as a Window into Human Nature*. Penguin.

Pinker, S., M. A. Nowak, and J. J. Lee. 2008. "The Logic of Indirect Speech." *Proceedings of the National Academy of Sciences* 105 (3): 833–838.

The Nonviolent Requests Guide

Hess, J. A. 2003. "Maintaining Undesired Relationships." In *Maintaining Relationships Through Communication: Relational, Contextual, and Cultural Variations*, edited by D. J. Canary and M. Dainton, 103–124. Lawrence Erlbaum Associates.

Kahane, A. 2017. *Collaborating with the Enemy: How to Work with People You Don't Agree with or Like or Trust*. Berrett-Koehler Publishers.

Marshall, R., and P. D. Rosenberg. 2003. *Nonviolent Communication: A Language of Life*. PuddleDancer Press.

McCracken, H. 2017. "Satya Nadella Rewrites Microsoft's Code." *Fast Company*. September 18.

Section 4: Dive Deeper

Mutual Understanding and Common Ground

Clark, H. H. 1996. *Using Language*. Cambridge University Press.

Clark, H. H., and S. E. Brennan. 1991. "Grounding in Communication." Perspectives on Socially *Shared Cognition* 13: 127–149.

De Freitas, J., K. Thomas, P. DeScioli, and S. Pinker. 2019. "Common Knowledge, Coordination, and Strategic Mentalizing in Human Social Life." *Proceedings of the National Academy of Sciences* 116 (28): 13751–13758.

Klein, G., P. J. Feltovich, J. M. Bradshaw, and D. D. Woods. 2005. "Common Ground and Coordination in Joint Activity." In *Organizational Simulation*, edited by W. B. Rouse and K. R. Boff, 139–184. John Wiley & Sons.

Mastrogiacomo, S., S. Missonier, and R. Bonazzi. 2014. "Talk Before It's Too Late: Reconsidering the Role of Conversation in Information Systems Project Management." *Journal of Management Information Systems* 31 (1): 47–78.

"Media Richness Theory." Wikipedia. https://en.wikipedia.org/w/index.php?title=Media_richness_theory&oldid=930255670

Trust and Psychological Safety

Edmondson, A. 1999. "Psychological Safety and Learning Behavior in Work Teams." *Administrative Science Quarterly* 44 (2): 350–383.

Edmondson, A. C. 2018. *The Fearless Organization: Creating Psychological Safety in the Workplace for Learning, Innovation, and Growth*. John Wiley & Sons.

Edmondson, A. C. 2004. "Psychological Safety, Trust, and Learning in Organizations: A Group-Level Lens." In *Trust and Distrust in Organizations: Dilemmas and Approaches*, edited by R. M. Kramer and K. S. Cook, 239–272. Russell Sage Foundation.

Edmondson, A. C., and A. W. Woolley, A. W. 2003. "Understanding Outcomes of Organizational Learning Interventions." In *International Handbook on Organizational Learning and Knowledge Management*, edited by M. Easterby-Smith and M. Lyles, 185–211. London: Blackwell.

Tucker, A. L., I. M. Nembhard, and A. C. Edmondson. 2007. "Implementing New Practices: An Empirical Study of Organizational Learning in Hospital Intensive Care Units." *Management Science* 53 (6): 894–907.

Face and Politeness

Brown, P., and S. C. Levinson. 1987. *Politeness: Some Universals in Language Usage*. Vol. 4. Cambridge University Press.

Culpeper, J. 2011. "Politeness and Impoliteness." In *Pragmatics of Society*, edited by W. Bublitz, A. H. Jucker, and K. P. Schneider. Vol. 5, 393. Mouton de Gruyter.

Fiske, A. P. 1992. "The Four Elementary Forms of Sociality: Framework for a Unified Theory of Social Relations." *Psychological Review* 99 (4): 689.

Kim, W., and R. Mauborgne. 1997. "Fair Process." *Harvard Business Review* 75: 65–75.

Lee, J. J., and S. Pinker. 2010. "Rationales for Indirect Speech: The Theory of the Strategic Speaker." *Psychological Review* 117 (3): 785.

Locher, M. A., and R. J. Watts, R. J. 2008. "Relational Work and Impoliteness: Negotiating Norms of Linguistic Behaviour." In *Impoliteness in Language. Studies on its Interplay with Power in Theory and Practice*, edited by D. Bousfield and M. A. Locher, 77–99. Mouton de Gruyter.

Pless, N., and T. Maak. 2004. "Building an Inclusive Diversity Culture: Principles, Processes and Practice." *Journal of Business Ethics* 54 (2): 129–147.

Pinker, S. 2007. *The Stuff of Thought: Language as a Window into Human Nature*. Penguin.

Pinker, S., M. A. Nowak, and J. J. Lee. 2008. "The Logic of Indirect Speech." *Proceedings of the National Academy of Sciences* 105, (3): 833–838.

Index

I

Impoliteness, 235
Incomplete facts, 213–214
Indirect request, 235
Informed decision making, 140–141
Initial alignment, in projects, 152–153
Initial TAM sessions, 156
Initiatives, transformation, 188–189
Inner dialogue, 249
Innovation:
    failure in, 203
    unsafe team climate undermining, 14–15
INSEAD, 286
Intelligent failures, 203
Interpretation, in Fact Finder, 210
Inventory of needs, 251
Irrelevant common ground, 13

J

Joint Commitment Ritual, 66
Joint commitments, 62–69
    analyzing, in Assessment Mode, 113
    defining, 66–67
    defining, in workspace, 50–51
    examples, 68–69
    in forward pass (example), 91, 95, 99
Joint objectives, 54–61
    analyzing, in Assessment Mode, 113
    defining, 58–59
    defining, in workspace, 50–51
    examples, 60–61
    in forward pass (example), 90, 94, 98
    negotiating and allocating resources
        for, 180

Joint resources, 70–77
    analyzing, in Assessment Mode, 113
    in backward pass (example), 92, 96, 100
    defining, 74–75
    defining, in workspace, 50–51
    examples, 76–77
    in forward pass (example), 91, 95, 99
Joint risks, 78–85
    analyzing, in Assessment Mode, 113
    in backward pass (example), 93, 97, 101
    defining, 82–83
    defining, in workspace, 50–51
    examples, 84–85
    in forward pass (example), 91, 95, 99
Judgments, 210, 213, 215

K

Kanban-stye TAM, 158–161
    about, 158–159
    in practice, 160–161
Kim, Cham, 286
Klein, G., 260
Kniberg, Henrik, 174
Kourilsky, Françoise, xi
KPIs, considering emotions as, 145

L

Lack of clarity, 144
Latecomers, managing, 145
Leaders:
    and cross-functional alignment, 179
    negotiating resources with, 180
    teams empowered by, 174
Lean UX cycle, 256

Learning, team, 14–15
Learning zone, 269
Letters, addressed, 265
Levinson, Stephen, 284
Limitations, 210, 213, 215
Low common ground, 13–14
Low team learning, 14
Low team performance, 14

M

Mauborgne, Renée, 286
Media types, for communication, 265
Meeting attendance, 246
Meetings, 132–145
    Assessment Mode for, 142–143
    boosting team engagement in, 136–137
    focusing the team in, 134–135
    increasing impact of, 138–139
    making informed decisions in, 140–141
    pro tips for, 144–145
    timebox, 134
    update, 145
    weekly TAM, 156–157
Mental Research Institute, xi
Microsoft, 242
Milestones, 166
Miro, 164
Misaligned relationship modes, 278–279
Misaligned team activities, signs of, 11
Missing stakeholders, managing, 145
Mission:
    describing your, 53
    in forward pass (example), 90, 94, 98
    importance of, 52
    repairing, 115

Acknowledgments

Book Team

This book is the result of a long journey involving a great many people and teams that helped us design, experiment, test, and improve the tools, and finally to design the content. We thank everyone for their individual contributions and patience during our endless workshops, repeated surveys, and rounds of unnecessary questions.

First, we thank the thousands of early adopters who used some of our early concepts and contributed to the evolution and refinement of the ideas we present here.

We are grateful to Stéphanie Missonier, Hazbi Avdiji, Yves Pigneur, Françoise Kourilsky, Adrian Bangerter, and Pierre Dillenbourg for the initial academic work and their unique contribution to the conceptual foundations of the tools. We thank many great field practitioners: Alain Giannattasio, Thomas Steiner, Yasmine Made, Renaud Litré, Antonio Carriero, Fernando Yepez, Jamie Jenkins, Gigi Lai, David Bland, Ivan Torreblanca, Sumayah Aljasem, Jose-Carlos Barbara, Eva Sandner, Koffi Kragba, and Julia van Graas for experimenting and helping improve our early prototypes and the manuscript. Thanks go to Pierre Sindelar, Tony Vogt, Monica Wagen, and Pascal Antoine for passionately challenging our ideas and findings, and to David Carroll for his great support when were struggling with the title.

We are indebted to our illustrators, Bernard Granger and Séverine Assous, for their dedication and the beauty of their artistic work, with a special thanks to Louise Ducatillon, who helped initiate this artistic collaboration, and to Trish Papadakos and Chris White, for the impressive design work they've accomplished. We are grateful to our publisher, Wiley, especially to Richard Narramore, Victoria Annlo, and Vicki Adang for the guidance and the improvements made to the manuscript. We also wish to thank all the great many collaborators at Strategyzer: Tom Philip, Jonas Baer, Federico Galindo, Przemek Kowalczyk, Mathias Maisberger, Kavi Guppta, Franziska Beeler, Niki Kotsonis, Jerry Steele, Tanja Oberst, Shamira Miller, Paweł Sułkowski, Aleksandra Czaplicka, Jon Friis, Frederic Etiemble, Matt Woodward, Silke Simons, Daniela Leutwyler, Gabriel Roy, Dave Thomas, Natlie Loots, Piotr Pawlik, Jana Stevanovic, Tendayi Viki, Janice Gallen, Andrew Martiniello, Lee Hockin, Laine McGarragle, Andrew Maffi, and Lucy Luo.

Finally, the book wouldn't be what it is without Honora Ducatillon, who relentlessly challenged, commented on, and encouraged each step of the editing process.

– Stefano, Alex, and Alan

Book Team

Lead Author
Stefano Mastrogiacomo

Stefano Mastrogiacomo is a management consultant, professor, and author. He has a passion for human coordination and he's the designer of the Team Alignment Map, the Team Contract, the Fact Finder, and the other tools presented in this book. He's been leading digital projects and advising project teams in international organizations for more than 20 years, while teaching and doing research at the University of Lausanne, Switzerland. His interdisciplinary work is anchored in project management, change management, psycholinguistics, evolutionary anthropology, and design thinking.

teamalignment.co

Author
Alex Osterwalder

Alex is a leading author, entrepreneur, and in-demand speaker whose work has changed the way established companies do business and how new ventures get started. Ranked No. 4 of the top 50 management thinkers worldwide, Alex also holds the Thinkers50 Strategy Award. Together with Yves Pigneur he invented the Business Model Canvas, the Value Proposition Canvas, and the Business Portfolio Map—practical tools that are trusted by millions of business practitioners.

@AlexOsterwalder
strategyzer.com/blog

Creative Lead
Alan Smith

Alan uses his curiosity and creativity to ask questions and turn the answers into simple, visual, practical tools. He believes that the right tools give people confidence to aim high and build big meaningful things. He cofounded Strategyzer with Alex Osterwalder, where he works with an inspired team to build great products. Strategyzer's books, tools, and services are used by leading companies around the world.

strategyzer.com

Design Lead
Trish Papadakos

Trish holds a Masters in Design from Central St. Martins in London and a Bachelor of Design from the York Sheridan Joint Program in Toronto.

She has taught design at her alma mater, worked with award-winning agencies, launched several businesses, and is collaborating for the seventh time with the Strategyzer team.

Designer
Chris White

Chris is a multidisciplinary designer who lives in Toronto. He has spent his time working on a number of business publications in various roles, most recently as Assistant Art Director at *The Globe and Mail*, focusing on presentation design for both print and online stories.

Illustrator
Severine Assous

Severine is a French illustrator based in Paris, working primarily on children's books, publications, and advertising. Her characters grace the pages of the book.

Illustrator
Blexbolex

Bernard Granger (Blexbolex) is an illustrator, comic book artist, and the 2009 recipient of the Golden Letter Award for best book design in the world. He created the image for the book's cover along with several pages throughout of humorous imaginings of contemporary office culture.

illustrissimo.fr

Strategyzer uses the best of technology and coaching to support your transformation and growth challenges.

Discover what we can do for you at Strategyzer.com

Create Growth Repeatedly
Systematize and scale your growth efforts, build an innovation culture, and broaden your pipeline of ideas and projects with Strategyzer Growth Portfolio.

Strategyzer is the global leader in growth and innovation services. We help companies around the world build new engines of growth based on our proven methodology and technology-enabled services.

Create Change at Scale
Build state-of-the-art business skills at scale with Strategyzer Academy and online coaching.

Strategyzer prides itself on designing the simplest and most applicable business tools. We help practitioners become more customer centric, design outstanding value propositions, find better business models, and align teams.